INDE

Coffee Book

SECOND **2** EDITION

LONDON

WORDS BY
Alex Evans & Derek Lamberton

PHOTOGRAPHY BY
Victor Frankowski

First published in the UK by Vespertine Press Ltd. 2013

Copyright Vespertine Press Ltd. 2013

A catalogue of this book is available from the British Library

ISBN 978-0-9566582-5-8

Design by Matt Barker at Artwerk.co.uk
Covers by Lloyd Price and Alex Evans
Digital mapping by Encompass Graphics Ltd., Hove, UK
encompass-graphics.co.uk

Printed and bound in the UK by

Set in Gotham & **U.S. 101**

Also available from Vespertine Press –
Craft Beer London
&
The Wellbeing Guide to London

www.vespertinepress.co.uk

CONTENTS

FOREWORD   6

ASSOCIATION   10
CURATORS COFFEE STUDIO   14
TAYLOR ST. BARISTAS – MONUMENT   16
PROTEIN BY DUNNEFRANKOWSKI   20
GIDDY UP FLORIPA   22
OZONE COFFEE   24
SALVATION JANE   26
LOOK MUM, NO HANDS   28
DOSE ESPRESSO   30
WORKSHOP COFFEE CO. – CLERKENWELL   32
PRUFROCK COFFEE   36
NOTES COFFEE BARROW   40
CENTRAL LISTINGS   42

Central

NOTES   46
ESPRESSO ROOM   48
RAPHA CYCLE CLUB   50
FLAT WHITE   52
T-A-P COFFEE   54
KAFFEINE   58
WORKSHOP COFFEE CO. – MARYLEBONE   60
WEST END LISTINGS   62

West End

East

NUDE ESPRESSO	68
SQUARE MILE COFFEE ROASTERS	70
CLIMPSON & SONS	74
46B ESPRESSO HUT	76
UNION HAND ROASTED	78
TAYLOR ST. BARISTAS – SOUTH QUAY	80
EAST LISTINGS	82

North

EMBASSY EAST	88
TINA, WE SALUTE YOU	90
CARAVAN KING'S CROSS	92
THE FIELDS BENEATH	96
VAGABOND N4	98
NORTH LISTINGS	100

South

CRAFT COFFEE	104
MONMOUTH COFFEE – DOCKLEY ROAD	106
DARK FLUID	108
BROWNS OF BROCKLEY	112
FEDERATION	114
BIRDHOUSE	118
SOUTH LISTINGS	120

Coffee Compendium

A HISTORY OF LONDON COFFEE HOUSES	124
COFFEE ROASTING	132
THE RISE OF LONDON COFFEE CARTS	136
BREWING GUIDES	141
GLOSSARY	149

MAPS	INSIDE BACK COVER

USING THIS GUIDE

The first part of this book serves as a guide to the cafés and coffee bars in London. They are divided into five key areas comprising Central, West End, East, North and South, allowing you to easily find these places depending on your location. At the end of each area section there are listings of other recommended speciality coffee shops that we highly suggest you visit.

There are three page styles distinguishing cafés, coffee carts and roasters, each containing key information such as train and bus routes, opening hours and contact details. (Please note: whilst we have done our very best to keep all of this information current, there may be unforeseeable changes made to these details during the lifespan of this book. If in doubt, contact the café or roaster directly and refer to the TFL website for changes to scheduled transport.)

The second part of this book is a Coffee Compendium, comprising information about coffee, its history and its place in London today. There are also in-depth brewing guides to get the most out of your coffee at home. Finally, at the back of the book you will find a fold-out map of London, detailing the areas both north and south of the River Thames.

The following logos appear throughout the guide. They denote:

Coffee Cart

Coffee Roaster

FOREWORD

by Ben Townsend
Espresso Room

In the last two years we have seen a huge growth in the scope and scale of London coffee. In most parts of central London now, a good coffee is close by; it's becoming more normal, as opposed to special.

Having started out as a culture that has been driven by independents, we're already seeing a shift into the mainstream. There are more cafés to go to, which means more people having access to them, and we're also seeing the spread of this culture into the national, high street fabric of the UK with high-profile collaborations between independents and big financial backers. This is an inevitable change in the style of business but I still believe that the London coffee scene is very much driven by an independent spirit, both in terms of quality, innovation and personality.

Most interestingly perhaps, London seems to be rapidly developing its own identity within speciality coffee, whereas previously, even when the first edition of this book was released in December 2011, the majority of cafés owed much of their standards, ideas and techniques to Australian and New Zealand coffee culture. Now, baristas from other cities – as diverse as Melbourne and Tokyo, for example - are deliberately coming to London to learn what is going on here. It has become much more common to see cafés staffed by baristas from all over the world, whether from Asia, Scandinavia, Europe or the US. London has now become a city where the availability of great coffee and the origin of the baristas more properly represents the multicultural personality of the city itself.

When compared with other cities around the world, especially those with a previously more evolved café or coffee culture, you can make a convincing argument that London now has the best and most interesting coffee scene in the world, and that's a huge development in a relatively short period of time.

With the explosion of change and offering we have seen in recent years, there is the risk of the industry outpacing the public's expectations, or our ability to communicate these new offerings effectively. For this reason I believe there is currently some confusion surrounding what makes a café different, what the quality standards must be and why price levels are as they are. It's already evident that tiers of quality are emerging, as in any mature industry: a trend that we have to explain intelligently.

As we progress, I hope that the more discriminating consumer will be prepared to pay a little more for the most outstanding coffee, which would allow cafés to pay their staff a better wage and to afford to buy even better roasted coffee. This would also mean that farmers would be paid more for their speciality grade crops and ensure that levels of quality continue to improve across the board. The most inhibiting factor for most cafés is money within the system and I expect to see, at some point, a higher cup price to enable an even higher quality of product to be served to the customer.

The London coffee scene would be nothing without its customers, so I sincerely thank you for supporting us, and recommend this new edition as an invaluable reference for enjoying the cutting edge of world coffee. I hope you enjoy the varied and distinctive offerings that are now available in this great city and beyond.

Coffee Hit

...The place to get all your coffee gear

ASSOCIATION

10-12 Creechurch Lane EC3A 5AY
www.associationcoffee.com
@AssociationEC3

Central

Hours	Mon-Fri: 7.30am - 5pm Sat & Sun: Closed	Wifi	Yes
Trains	Aldgate	Credit cards	Yes
Buses	100, 135, 205, 42, 78 Duke's Place	Alcohol	No
		W.C.	Yes
		Outdoor seating	No

Beans	Square Mile, Has Bean, Workshop	Grinders	Mazzer Robur E, Mazzer Kony, Anfim Caimano, Mahlkönig Tanzania
Machine	Synesso 'Hydra'		

Alternative brewing methods V60, Aeropress, Siphon

Ask any barista in London where to drink excellent coffee and more often than not they will point you to David Robson at Association. After a period honing his skills at Prufrock and elsewhere, Robson has brought an unrivaled passion to this remarkable coffee shop, known officially as The Association: City of London Coffee Project.

Robson and Association's baristas produce exquisitely crafted coffee - easily ranking amongst the capital's best. Their skill and dedication to quality is apparent in each cup and the staff, serving beans from Square Mile, Has Bean and Workshop on a Synesso or along the impressive brew bar, attract an interesting mix of coffee connoisseurs. Indeed, Association is perhaps unusual in that both buttoned-up bankers and trendy East Londoners feel at home here. Regardless of their interests, visitors find themselves admiring the remarkable latte art and impressive interior.

The café design - by Melbourne-based Herbert & Mason - is London's most striking. The unusual dark olive rubber surface of the bar retreats into subdued lighting, creating a spartan atmosphere which is neatly parallelled by the baristas' no-nonsense approach to coffee. The designers of the café sought to respond to both the original character of The Old Tea Warehouse, which houses Association, and the ever-shifting City surrounding it. The exposed brick and steel frame of the warehouse is thus juxtaposed with the aforementioned rubber surfaces alongside geometrically designed furniture and table tops. The design, despite its allure, manages to support rather than distract from the coffee experience.

In the morning, the café serves a simple yet tasty breakfast menu along with a variety of pastries and treats throughout the day from artisan bakers such as Bittersweet, Little Bread Peddler and St John Bakery. Sandwiches are freshly produced for lunch with meats from the Food Collective and cheeses from Neal's Yard Dairy. As the quality of the suppliers suggest, everything is thoughtfully produced and delicious.

The arrival of The Association: City of London Coffee Project marks a turning point in London's café scene. The level of quality displayed here firmly places speciality coffee in the upper echelons of London's now world-renowned food culture. Association has in many respects raised the bar but more importantly it has offered a new vision of an independent coffee shop - one in which quality is utterly uncompromised.

CURATORS COFFEE STUDIO

9 Cullum Street EC3M 7JJ
www.curatorscoffee.com
@Curators_Coffee

Central

Hours	Mon-Fri: 7.30am - 5pm Sat & Sun: Closed	Wifi	No	
		Credit cards	Yes	
Trains	Monument	Alcohol	No	
Buses	149, 344, 35, 47, 48 Fenchurch Street	W.C.	No	
		Outdoor seating	Yes	
Beans	Union Hand Roasted, Square Mile	Grinders	Mazzer Robur E, Anfim Super Caimano, Mazzer Mini	
Machine	La Marzocco 'Strada' EP			

Curators Coffee Studio is nothing short of a haven within the complex topography of the City. Visitors are met by an attractive collection of custom teal-plated coffee machinery - including the star attraction of a La Marzocco Strada - expertly handled by Catherine and her team. This being a café in the City, the focus is squarely on espresso with Union's Rogue blend served daily alongside guest espressos from Square Mile and other roasters. Croissants arrive fresh every morning from Yeast Bakery along with cake from Bittersweet Bakers and toasted sandwiches are available at lunchtime.

The café, as the name suggests, is studio-sized, but the tall windows and high ceiling, combined with the soft grey wall, create an impression of space and a sensation of calm. The collection of wonderful illustrations casually decorating the café, not to mention the evident skill and approachable manner of the staff, make Curators a unique getaway - and a place worth visiting again and again.

TAYLOR ST. BARISTAS
MONUMENT

2 Botolph Alley EC3R 8DR
www.taylor-st.com
@Taylor_St

Central				
Hours	Weds-Fri: 10am – 7pm		Wifi	Yes
	Sat & Sun: 10am – 5pm		Credit cards	Yes
Trains	Monument		Alcohol	No
Buses	133, 141, 149, 17, 21, 35		W.C.	Yes
	Monument Station		Outdoor seating	No

Beans	Various	Grinder	Mahlkönig Tanzania
Machine	N/A		
Alternative brewing methods		V60, Clever Dripper, Aeropress, Cafétiere	

Taylor St. Baristas is without doubt one of London's coffee success stories. When Nick, Laura and Andrew Tolley arrived from Sydney back in 2006, London coffee was in a sorry state of affairs. Now, and with nine speciality coffee shops to their name, the sibling trio have helped change the face of the capital's coffee drinking habits and raised the standard we have come to expect around the city.

Although Taylor St. carry a regularly updated list of guest espresso and single origin coffees, their house Rogue espresso blend is the mainstay of the coffee menu and was developed in collaboration between Union Hand Roasted and Taylor St.'s very own Andrew Tolley. Designed to be an unconventional and ever changing blend, Rogue's components are

16

adjusted to incorporate some of the best seasonal lots, but is kept sweet and balanced in the roast and then consistently extracted by baristas throughout their cafés. It means that whether joining the coffee queue that trails from the doorway of the New St. espresso bar, lunching in their swish Mayfair café or enjoying the unusual surrounds of what can only be described as their Shoreditch coffee shed, you can be sure that whenever you see Taylor St.'s name, the coffee you receive will be consistently high grade.

With the Monument gallery, Andrew and his team have sought to create a coffee exhibition space, offering an exploration of coffee not found in your every day café experience. For this reason there is no espresso, milk or takeaway cups served at Taylor St. Monument – if it's a regular flat white you're after you'll need to make the short trip north to Curators or Association. But what this café does offer in its place is arguably more appealing. Showcasing seasonal coffees and micro-lots, roasted by both Union and other London speciality names, in a variety of different brewing methods and serving vessels, Taylor St. Monument offers a journey of sensory exploration, as much informative as it is enjoyable. In addition, Monument also houses a state-of-the-art training centre downstairs, where new coffee recruits hone their skills in public and professional training sessions, and Taylor St.'s already battle-hardened baristas can perfect their art.

PROTEIN
BY DUNNEFRANKOWSKI

18 Hewett Street EC2A 3NN
www.dunnefrankowski.com
@DunneFrankowski

Hours	Mon-Fri: 8am-5pm	Wifi	Yes
	Sat & Sun: Coffee classes by appointment	Credit cards	Yes
Trains	Shoreditch High Street	Alcohol	No
Buses	135, 35, 388, 47, 8	W.C.	Yes
	Shoreditch High Street Station	Outdoor seating	Yes
Beans	Various	Grinders	Anfim Milano, Mahlkönig Tanzania
Machine	Cimbali 'M39' HD		
Alternative brewing methods	Technivorm Moccamaster		

Rob Dunne and Victor Frankowski are the creative force behind one of London's most original coffee bars on the ground floor of a creative agency in Shoreditch. The duo, who met a few years ago as baristas at the newly opened Tapped and Packed, combined forces to inspire a more thorough understanding of speciality coffee amongst both their customers and the industry as a whole. Through their self-titled creative coffee company, the two have become a ubiquitous and disruptive presence in London, challenging the status quo while continuing to engage with coffee drinkers at their popular cupping classes and coffee bar. The bar itself is entirely dedicated to coffee with what is certainly London's widest selection of beans on rotation. Expect to find beans from the UK's most respected roasters alongside coffees roasted in Scandinavia, Australia, North America and elsewhere.

GIDDY UP FLORIPA

93 Great Eastern Street EC2A 3HZ
@GiddyUpFloripa

Central

Hours	Mon: 7.30am - 4pm Tues-Sun: 7.30am - 10pm	Wifi	Yes
		Credit cards	No
Trains	Old Street	Alcohol	Yes
Buses	135, 243, 55 - Old Street Station	W.C.	Yes
		Outdoor seating	Yes
Beans	Various	Machine	Kees van der Westen 'Mirage' Idrocompresso
Grinder	Mazzer Robur E		
Alternative brewing methods	V60, Aeropress		

Showcasing one of two Kees van der Westen lever machines within a quarter of a mile, Giddy Up's cart at Floripa is easily one of the best places to learn about coffee in the capital. On most mornings you will find the barista dialing in one of a variety of coffees underneath the orange awning of Floripa - a Brazilian themed restaurant that the cart shares space with. Using beans from James Gourmet, Square Mile, Has Bean, Workshop and a seemingly endless rotation of guest roasters from around the world, the coffee is expertly served from the lever machine or through a variety of filter methods.

Croissants by Yeast Bakery are available to accompany your morning coffee and thanks to the relationship with Floripa there is plenty of seating. In the late afternoon, after a brief break, the cart is re-positioned within the restaurant where Giddy Up continues to provide top flight coffee until 10pm. Look out for occasional late evening cocktail collaborations such as a summertime favourite featuring cold brew coffee and sloe gin.

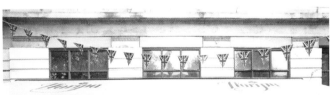

OZONE COFFEE

11 Leonard Street EC2A 4AQ
www.ozonecoffee.co.uk
@OzoneCoffee

Hours	Mon-Fri: 7.30am - 5pm Sat & Sun: 9am - 4pm	Wifi	Yes
Trains	Old Street	Credit cards	Yes
Buses	141, 205, 21, 214, 43, 76 Leonard Street	Alcohol	Yes
		W.C.	Yes
		Outdoor seating	No

Beans	Ozone Coffee	Grinders	Mazzer Robur E x3, Mazzer Major E, Mazzer Super Jolly E
Machine	Synesso 'Hydra', Nuova Simonelli 'Aurelia' T3		

Alternative brewing methods V60, Aeropress, Siphon, Woodneck

Ozone Coffee Roasters have been an established name in New Zealand's speciality circles for 15 years, not least in their home surfing town of Fitzroy, New Plymouth. In London the company made waves in March 2012 by opening a vast café roastery a stones throw from Old Street roundabout. In truth, it took the roasting side of the business a few months to find its feet but it has since come into its own. Head roaster James Gurr works on a Probat UG22, which is housed in the basement of the warehouse-style café, along with a sate-of-the-art training facility. Whilst the coffee menu rightly grabs your attention, the food options at Ozone are also well worth exploring and reasonably priced too, when you consider that this is prime London real estate. The Honest to Goodness - a brunch consisting of a soft boiled egg, toast & preserves, vanilla bean yoghurt with berries and juice - is the perfect pre or post-coffee meal.

SALVATION JANE

Unit 2, 1 Oliver's Yard, 55 City Road EC1Y 1HQ
www.salvationjanecafe.co.uk
@salvationjaneUK

Central				
Hours	Mon: 7.30am - 4pm Tues-Fri: 7.30am - 11pm Sat & Sun: 9am - 4pm	W.C.	Yes
		Wifi	Yes
		Alcohol	Yes
Trains	Old Street	Credit cards	Yes
Buses	141, 205, 21, 214, 43, 76 - City Road	Outdoor seating	Yes
Beans	Square Mile	Grinders	Mazzer Robur E x2
Machine	La Marzocco FB-80		

At first glance, Lantana's newer sister café Salvation Jane has little in common with its predecessor, aside from the attractive illustrated mural of plants and flowers that climbs the expanse of far wall in the restaurant area. However, on closer inspection, all the hallmarks of Shelagh Ryan's previous enterprise become clear, from the emphasis on expertly made coffee, to the Aussie inspired menu with its beautiful brunch-style dishes. The space itself is large and in the 'warehouse chic' category - something London has become used to in recent years - though Salvation Jane is slick without feeling cold and unwelcoming. The quirks reminiscent of Lantana give the café an endearing and familiar feel, alike the baristas and service team who are friendly and attentive.

A Salvation Jane is a type of hardy plant iconic in Australia and renowned for its survival during drought. If the success of these first two cafés is anything to go by, then it may not be the last of Shelagh's cafés to take root in recession hit London.

LOOK MUM, NO HANDS

49 Old Street EC1V 9HX
www.lookmumnohands.com
@1ookmumnohands

Hours	Mon-Fri: 7.30am - 10pm		Wifi		Yes
	Sat: 9am - 10pm		Credit cards		Yes
	Sun: 9.30am - 10pm				
Trains	Old Street		Alcohol		Yes
Buses	55, 243, N35, N55		W.C.		Yes
	Aldersgate Street		Outdoor seating		Yes
Beans	Square Mile + regular guest espresso		Grinders	Anfim Super Caimano x2, Mazzer Super Jolly	
Machine	Kees Van Der Westen 'Mirage'				
Alternative brewing methods	Clever Dripper				

Central

The popularity of London's first dedicated cycle café has yet to wane, despite the arrival in the city of several other' similarly velocentric establishments in the past year. Cycling has become cool again, fuelled in no small part by the success of British riders in 2012's Olympics and the Tour de France, possibly the café's busiest events on the big screen to date. But the loyal following is also due to the coffee they serve, which remains consistently good, with Square Mile shots now pulled on a gorgeous Kees Van Der Westen and offered as pour over at the bar. The café also now boasts its very own take-away coffee cart in the adjacent yard, utilizing a customised genuine ex-army Tornado repair cart. The welcome addition of more craft beer from Bristol Beer Factory, Partizan and Williams Brothers into Look Mum's fridges, adding to the bottles from the Kernel Brewery, also make for the perfect post-cycle refreshment.

DOSE ESPRESSO

70 Long Lane EC1A 9EJ
www.dose-espresso.com
@dose_espresso

Central

Hours	Mon-Fri: 7am - 5pm Sat: 9am - 4pm	W.C.	No
		Wifi	Yes
Trains	Barbican	Alcohol	No
Buses	56, 153, 4 Barbican Station	Credit cards	Yes
		Outdoor seating	Yes

Beans	Square Mile	Grinders	Ceado E92, Anfim Super Caimano, Mahlkönig Vario
Machine	La Marzocco 'FB-80'		

Alternative brewing methods Aeropress, Clever Dripper

Having manned the Climpson & Sons coffee cart for two years and worked in the Sydney coffee industry for seven years prior, James Phillips had become one of London's speciality coffee pioneers long before the city had much of a clue about good coffee. His café, Dose, still remains one of the few reliable stopping points for a consistently great espresso, that's despite being dwarfed in stature by many of the giant new breed of London's coffee barns. This consistency is down as much to James' straightforward approach to coffee and service - a character trait echoed in the fact that very little has changed at Dose since it opened in 2009 - as it is to the fact that Dose was one of Square Mile's first wholesale clients, an alliance reflected by the shared red, black and white colour scheme that prevails in the café. It's a partnership that has since led to a collaboration with Google Campus in Shoreditch, where Dose serves as the resident on-site coffee shop providing some of London's brightest start-ups with their daily caffeine fix.

WORKSHOP COFFEE CO.
CLERKENWELL

27 Clerkenwell Road EC1M 5RN
www.workshopcoffee.com
@WorkshopCoffee

Central

Hours	Mon: 7.30am - 6pm Tues-Fri: 7.30am - 10pm Sat & Sun: 8am - 6pm	Wifi	No
		Credit cards	Yes
		Alcohol	Yes
Trains	Farringdon	W.C.	Yes
Buses	153, 243, 55 Clerkenwell Road	Outdoor seating	Yes

Beans	Workshop	Grinders	Mazzer Robur E x3, Mazzer Major E, Mahlkönig Tanzania
Machine	Synesso 'Cyncra', La Marzocco 'Linea'		

Alternative brewing methods Aeropress

Having changed names and undergone an overhaul of the company infrastructure less than a year after landing in London, most other coffee shops would have struggled to maintain their composure. Not so Workshop Coffee Co. Under its former guise as St. Ali - the Melbourne-based speciality coffee and food purveyors - the opening of this Clerkenwell café roastery in 2011 caused a stir, not least for its size and good looks but also as it was the first major UK outpost of any Australian coffee company.

The ship-steadying influence behind Workshop is Director of Operations Tim Williams. His years of experience working with St. Ali in Melbourne, Intelligensia in L.A. and Square Mile in London make him one of the most qualified coffee professionals in the UK. Furthermore, his skill and fine eye for detail shine through in Workshop's output, whether that be in regards to the food, the coffee menu or, indeed, the company's expanding coffee roasting operation.

The wholesale roasting side of Workshop has well and truly found its feet in the last year, supplying other great independent cafés, like Embassy East, with their coffees. Their output includes the ever present Cult of Done espresso, alongside fine coffees from around the world which are hand roasted on a gleaming Probat at the back of the café, faced by a living wall of plants and flowers that scales the adjacent wall. Workshop's online 'Dispensary' offers their roasted coffee by the bag or by six or twelve month subscriptions, along with a solid selection of brewing hardware that will help to ensure the delicate flavours of coffee continue over into your own home brewing experiments.

Workshop's recent acquisition of James Bailey, who manned the brew bar at Prufrock Coffee for several years and was a 2012 World Brewer's Cup Finalist in Vienna, should certainly ensure that levels of quality continue across the board. To compliment the expert coffee offering that baristas like Bailey afford, the food served at Workshop is as conscientiously sourced and prepared as anything found in the hopper or at the brew bar. Brunch-style meals are to the fore, with dishes including baked organic eggs and corn fritters amongst the wholesome menu. Workshop is also open into the evening where both bar snacks and more adventurous dishes are served, such as ocean trout or Thai beef salad, alongside fine wines and craft beers from the Kernel and Camden Town Brewery.

PRUFROCK COFFEE

23-25 Leather Lane EC1N 7TE
www.prufrockcoffee.com
@PrufrockCoffee

Central

Hours	Mon-Fri: 8am - 6pm Sat & Sun: 10am - 5pm	Wifi	Yes
		Credit cards	Yes
Trains	Chancery Lane / Farringdon	Alcohol	No
		W.C.	Yes
Buses	17, 341, 45, 46 Holborn Circus	Outdoor seating	Yes

Beans	Square Mile	Grinders	Mahlkönig K30, Simonelli Mythos, Mazzer Robur E, Mahlkönig Tanzania
Machines	Victoria Arduino 'Athena Leva', Nuova Simmonelli T3, Kees Van Der Westen 'Spirit' & 'Speedster'		

Alternative brewing methods V60, Aeropress, Siphon

Somebody recently joked that Prufrock is the Manchester United of the speciality coffee industry. While the contradictory nature of this statement is obvious, it does have quite a lot of truth to it. The level of talent and skill found at both Prufrock's Leather Lane mothership and its pop up coffee bar in Shoreditch is nothing short of extraordinary. Those keeping score know that over the past few years the crew at Prufrock have collectively gathered a remarkable number of awards and accolades; some individual, such as James Bailey's recent win at the UK Brewer's Cup Championship, and others shared, like being awarded the 2012 Best Independent Coffee Shop at the European Coffee Symposium.

Surprisingly, considering the potential for pretension, Prufrock is one of the most relaxed coffee shops in London. Located on Clerkenwell's bustling Leather Lane, the interior is spacious and the atmosphere is playful. Visitors are met by one of London's first dedicated brew bars, the world's most memorably decorated espresso machine and a series of surprisingly pink columns.

The brew bar offers a daily menu, often with multiple beans roasted by the UK and the world's most influential roasters. It is an excellent spot to learn about coffee, from both Prufrock's baristas and the customers, who often bring a wide range of knowledge themselves. Occasionally there are also off-menu beans hidden under the bar so be sure to ask.

The espresso drinks, which are equally as good, are most often pulled on a Nuova Simonelli T3. The machine's casing is canvas to a remarkable painting by Martin Kingdom depicting an "alternative theory on the origins of coffee". Complete with pilgrims, pyramids and what appears to be an albino giraffe - all seemingly unaware of the enormous coffee bean-meteorite flashing through the sky - the narrative is wonderfully wacky yet it makes for what is undoubtedly the most original coffee machine ever seen. For those that prefer a more traditional approach, there is a beautiful lever-operated Victoria Arduino Athena Leva machine behind the bar - not to mention a pair of Kees Van Der Westens.

Putting their treasure chest of machinery to further use, Prufrock is home to a variety of training courses geared towards both aspiring professionals and home brewers known as BRAT (Barista Resource & Training). Courses are open to all and are taught by the team's championship-calibre staff, including owners Gwilym Davies and Jeremy Challender.

NOTES
COFFEE BARROW

186A Fleet Street EC4A 2HR
www.notes-uk.co.uk
@NotesBarrows

Central

Hours	Mon-Fri: 8am - 4.30pm	Buses	11, 15, 172, 23, 26, 341
	Sat & Sun: Closed		Chancery Lane
Trains	Chancery Lane / City Thameslink		

| Beans | Square Mile | Grinders | Anfim Caimano |
| Machine | La Marzocco 'FB-80' | | |

The coffee cart has become something of a mainstay of London's streets in previous years, providing a more than welcome alternative for an on the go coffee break than the chain café or, indeed, the ubiquitous burger van. Kings amongst this new culture are the growing fleet of Notes Coffee Barrows (previously Flat Cap) which are owned and operated by the good folk behind the renowned Notes cafés. This means that the quality of the coffee is guaranteed, whichever of their immaculate, gypsy-style carts you happen to visit. The Fleet Street outpost in particular, has all the virtues a good coffee cart should: namely fantastic coffee, friendly chat from the barista - even when it is freezing cold outdoors - and a fine location.

It's perhaps the latter of these points that sets the Fleet Street location apart from most, positioned as it is in the grounds of the beautiful 19th century St. Dunstan-in-the-West church. By way of factual touristic information, the impressive church clock that looms above the courtyard dates back to 1671 and was the first public timepiece in London to have a functioning minute hand. Not bad for a humble coffee cart.

Central

OTHER CENTRAL SPECIALITY COFFEE LOCATIONS

BEA'S OF BLOOMSBURY (ST. PAUL'S)

83 Watling Street London EC4M 9BX
Mon-Fri: 8am - 9pm, **Sat & Sun:** 12pm - 7pm
Trains: St. Paul's
Buses: 11, 23, 26, 388, 76 – Bank
www.beasofbloomsbury.com
@beas_bloomsbury

TAYLOR ST. BARISTAS (BANK)

125 Old Broad Street EC2N 1AR
Mon-Fri: 7am - 6pm, **Sat & Sun:** Closed
Trains: Bank / Liverpool Street
Buses: 242, 26, 388, 8 – Old Broad Street
www.taylor-st.com
@Taylor_St_Bank

TAYLOR ST. BARISTAS (LIVERPOOL STREET)

1A New Street EC2M 4TP
Mon-Fri: 7am - 5pm, **Sat:** Closed, **Sun:** 10am - 4pm
Trains: Liverpool Street
Buses: 149, 344, 35, 47, 48 – Liverpool Street Station
www.taylor-st.com
@Taylor_St_NewSt

FARM COLLECTIVE

91 Cowcross Street, Farringdon EC1M 6BH
Mon-Fri: 7am - 3.30pm, **Sat & Sun:** Closed
Trains: Farringdon
Buses: 17, 45, 63 – Snow Hill
www.farmcollective.com

GIDDY UP

Fortune Street Park EC1Y
Mon-Fri: 8am - 4:30pm, **Sat & Sun:** 10am - 4pm
Trains: Barbican
Buses: 153, 4, 56 – Barbican Station
@GiddyUpCoffee

DEPARTMENT OF COFFEE
& SOCIAL AFFAIRS

14-16 Leather Lane EC1N 7SU
Mon-Fri: 7am - 6pm, **Sat & Sun:** 10am - 5pm
Trains: Chancery Lane / Farringdon
Buses: 242, 25, 521, 8 – Chancery Lane Station
www.departmentofcoffee.co.uk
@DeptOfCoffee

FIX COFFEE

161 Whitecross Street, Shoreditch EC1Y 8JL
Mon-Fri: 7am - 7pm, **Sat:** 8am - 7pm, **Sun:** 9am - 7pm
Trains: Old Street
Buses: 243, 55 – St. Luke's
www.fix-coffee.co.uk

TAYLOR ST. BARISTAS (SHOREDITCH)

110 Clifton Street, Shoreditch EC2A 4HT
Mon-Fri: 8am - 5pm, **Sat & Sun:** Closed
Trains: Shoreditch High Street / Old Street
Buses: 35, 47, 78, 135 – Curtain Road
www.taylor-st.com
@Taylorst_shed

THE SHOREDITCH GRIND

213 Old Street EC1V 9NR
Mon-Thurs: 7am - 11pm, **Fri:** 7am - 1am, **Sat:** 9am - 1am,
Sun: 10am - 11pm
Trains: Old Street
Buses: 135, 243, 55 – Old Street Station
www.shoreditchgrind.com
@Shoreditchgrind

CARAVAN

11-13 Exmouth Market EC1R 4QD
Mon-Fri: 8am - 10.30pm, **Sat & Sun:** 10am - 10.30pm
Trains: Farringdon
Buses: 19, 38, 341 – Mount Pleasant
www.caravanonexmouth.co.uk
@CaravanExmouth

FIX 126

126 Curtain Road, Shoreditch EC2A 3PJ
Mon-Fri: 7am - 7pm, **Sat & Sun:** 8am - 7pm
Trains: Shoreditch High Street / Old Street
Buses: 35, 47, 78 – Curtain Road
www.fix-coffee.co.uk

NOTES

31 St. Martin's Lane WC2N 4ER
www.notes-uk.co.uk
@NotesTrafSq

West End

Hours	Mon-Weds: 7.30am-9pm Thurs & Fri: 7.30am-10pm Sat: 9am-10pm Sun: 10am-6pm	Wifi	No
		Credit cards	Yes
		Alcohol	Yes
		W.C.	Yes
Trains	Charing Cross	Outdoor seating	Yes
Buses	176, 24, 29 St Martin's Place		

Beans	Square Mile	Grinders	Mazzer Robur E, Anfim Super Caimano, Mahlkönig Tanzania
Machine	La Marzocco 'Strada'		

Alternative brewing methods Aeropress, V60, Cloth Filter

Fabio Ferreira and Robert Robinson have come a long way since they started up their Flat Cap Coffee cart on Strutton Ground. First there was the move to open this, their first café in the heart of theatre land - a homage to coffee that is still regarded as one of the finest speciality cafés in the West End - which was shortly followed by another similarly expert coffee shop in nearby Covent Garden. Simultaneously, the origin of the whole enterprise has grown into a fleet of five carts, now working under the banner of Notes Coffee Barrows, and which keep the cold and work weary tribes in good coffee and friendly banter, whatever the weather Furthermore, the business partners have designs on starting up their own coffee roasting division in the near future too. Watch this space.

ESPRESSO ROOM

31-35 Great Ormond Street WC1N 3HZ
www.theespressoroom.com
@theespressoroom

West End

Hours	Mon-Fri: 7.30am - 5pm Sat: 9.30am - 2.30pm	Wifi	No
		Credit cards	Yes
Trains	Russell Square	Alcohol	No
Buses	19, 243, 38, 55 Red Lion Square	W.C.	No
		Outdoor seating	Yes

Beans	Square Mile, Round Hill, Has Bean	Grinders	Mazzer Robur E, Mahlkönig Tanzania, Mahlkönig Vario x2, Ceado E37
Machine	Synesso 'Cyncra'		

Alternative brewing methods Batch brew filter

The Espresso Room is as pure a representation of the modern day, speciality coffee shop as you're likely to find. This is because, for all the million pound fit-outs, warehouse size seating areas and fine dining, the message can become a little diluted. This pocket battleship, situated across the road from Great Ormond Street Hospital, more than makes up for its diminutive dimensions with a quality focus that a larger café might struggle to match. Expert baristas maximise the space beautifully, pulling shots of Square Mile and Has Bean and working the queue that snakes from the doorway on a daily basis with a friendly familiarity. Owner Ben Townsend is as knowledgeable about London coffee as they come and regularly heads up coffee training courses around the UK. The formula he prescribes is that of simplicity and consistency, especially with regards his coffee. It's this ethos that makes the Espresso Room arguably the best pound-for-pound coffee shop in the whole of London.

RAPHA CYCLE CLUB

85 Brewer Street WC1 9ZN
www.rapha.cc
@RaphaRacing

West End

Hours	Mon-Fri: 7.30am - 9pm	WC	Yes
	Sat: 8.30am - 7pm	Wifi	Yes
	Sun: 10am - 6pm	Alcohol	No
Trains	Piccadilly Circus		
Buses	12, 159, 3, 453, 88, 94	Credit Cards	Yes
	Piccadilly Circus	Outdoor seating	No
Beans	JB Kaffee, Square Mile	Grinder	Anfim Super Caimano
Machine	Synesso 'Hydra'		

Spearheaded by places like Look Mum No Hands and Prufrock at Present, the relationships between speciality coffee and both cycling and retail have reached their pinnacle in Rapha Cycle Club's remarkable Brewer Street location. Well established now as a top notch clothing brand for cyclists, Rapha has brought their uncompromising quality and design-led approach to their in-house coffee bar, billed as a meeting place for road riders.

Determined to create a distinctive experience, Rapha hired the services of Paul Bonna from Frankfurt's Kaffee Kommune. Paul brought an unsurpassed level of coffee expertise to Brewer Street, training the staff on the brew bar and the remarkable customised Synesso with beans from JB Kaffee and Square Mile. Now led by Will, an ace barista well-known to many from Prufrock, Rapha Cycle Club is amongst the top tier of London coffee houses. Testament to Paul's influence is both the continued success of the coffee bar and the regular sighting of Johannes Bayer's JB Kaffee coffee beans across London's leading cafés.

FLAT WHITE

17 Berwick Street, Soho W1F 0PT
www.flatwhitecafe.com

West End

Hours	Mon-Fri: 8am - 7pm Sat & Sun: 9am - 6pm	Wifi	No
		Credit cards	No
Trains	Piccadilly Circus	Alcohol	No
Buses	22, 55, 7, 98 Wardour Street	W.C.	No
		Outdoor seating	Yes
Beans	Square Mile	Grinders	Mazzer Robur E, Anfim Super Caimano
Machine	Synesso 'Hydra'		

It's hard to imagine that when Flat White opened on Berwick Street in 2005 it was the only speciality coffee shop in Soho, perhaps even the whole of central London. The transformation that the capital's coffee landscape has undergone since has seen the flat white become a feature of British nomenclature and this little café go from strength to strength. The years between have also seen a change of ownership at both Flat White and similarly impressive sister café Milkbar on nearby Bateman Street, with founder member Cameron McClure moving back to his native New Zealand in 2012 after many years in the London coffee industry. But never fear: neither venue has suffered the loss of McClure's expertise or sunny disposition too greatly and both shops, using their own bespoke Square Mile blend, continue to serve some of the best espresso in this part of town. Furthermore, as a genus for the UK's growing number of speciality coffee shops, Flat White is up there with some of the most influential names in the world.

T-A-P COFFEE

193 Wardour Street, Soho W1F 8ZF
www.tapcoffee.co.uk
@tapcoffee

West End

Hours	Mon-Fri: 8am - 7pm Sat: 10am - 6pm	Wifi	Yes	
		Credit cards	Yes	
Trains	Tottenham Court Road	Alcohol	No	
Buses	10, 390, 73, 8 N73, N8 Wardour Street	W.C.	Yes	
		Outdoor seating	No	
Beans	T-A-P + guest coffees	Grinders	Mazzer Robur E	
Machine	Nuova Simonelli 'Aurelia'			
Alternative brewing methods	V60, Aeropress			

When the first Tapped & Packed café opened on Rathbone Place in 2009, it was one of the first to stock and brew coffees from an array of different roasters. That being a time when finding a café serving speciality coffee at all, let alone such an interesting or varied selection, rapidly made it one of Fitzrovia's most cherished places. The success of this first venue necessitated a second, which opened on Tottenham Court Road shortly afterwards. Similarly, this café cornered the market for good coffee in a criminally under represented area of central London, and maintained the sleek finishing and attentive design features of its predecessor. Now, under the new abbreviated name T-A-P, the company has begun roasting their own coffee in the back of their third and largest venue to date - a fine representation of the growth they have achieved in only a relatively short time.

The man tasked with overseeing T-A-P's foray into coffee roasting is Matthew Robley-Siemonsma, a former UKBC and Brewer's Cup entrant who has been with the company for several years in the capacity of manager. Having tested, sample roasted and cupped hundreds of coffees, the first of their roasted batches hit the shelves in April 2013. Consisting of lots chosen for their quality and diversity, the first T-A-P showcase of single origins included coffees from Ethiopia, Brazil and Columbia, along with their new house espresso blend, all bagged up in some of the nicest packaging we've laid eyes on.

Of course, having the space to do this helps and T-A-P Wardour Street has this in abundance. The roaster itself is positioned towards the far end of the ample space, beyond a counter on either side of the café: one stacked with gorgeous looking salads and sandwiches, all freshly made on site; the other manned by baristas making both filter brewed coffees and espresso. This may be a slightly unconventional and potentially confusing arrangement but the T-A-P staff are well versed in making you feel welcome. Another aspect which promotes familiarity is the trademark decor, which is pleasingly in tune with their other two shops and the overall T-A-P aesthetic. The old bike suspended above the doorway, the vintage demitasse spoons, Lyle syrup cans and the custom made benches are details that have all been referenced by a host of other cafés looking to match T-A-P's success. Imitation is the highest form of flattery, after all.

57

KAFFEINE

66 Great Titchfield Street, Fitzrovia W1W 7QJ
www.kaffeine.co.uk
@KaffeineLondon

West End

Hours	Mon-Fri: 7.30am – 6pm Sat: 8.30am – 6pm Sun: 9.30am - 5pm	Wifi	No
		Credit cards	Yes
Trains	Oxford Circus	Alcohol	No
Buses	12, 3, 453, 88, C2 Margaret Street	W.C.	Yes
		Outdoor seating	Yes
Beans	Square Mile + regular guest coffees	Grinders	Mazzer Robur E, Anfim Super Caimano
Machine	Synesso 'Cyncra'		

O pened in 2009, Kaffeine was one of the first to establish a reputation around the expertise of its baristas and has been using Square Mile's espresso blends from the outset, garnering 5 star reviews along the way as well as accolades, such as the title of Best Independent Café at the Café Society Awards 2012. Built on staples of great coffee and fine food, owner Peter Dore-Smith's two decades in the service industry translate into a café rich with subtle nuances which combine to create an overall impression of reliable quality. Kaffeine also runs monthly coffee courses, which focus on teaching all-comers the basics of home brewing and latte art, whilst also offering two hour, one-on-one tutorials, designed to get you familiar with making coffee on their Synesso.

In a similar vein to the attention given to coffee, all of the food sold here is produced on site with ingredients sourced from local vendors, specialist suppliers and independent market traders. Expect sumptuous salads, superb focaccia and filled baguettes alongside a host of delicious sweets, including the ever popular Anzac biscuits. All come highly recommended.

WORKSHOP COFFEE CO.
MARYLEBONE

75 Wigmore Street, Marylebone W1U 1QD
www.workshopcoffee.com
@WorkshopCoffee

West End

Hours	Mon-Fri: 7am - 5pm Sat & Sun: 10am - 5pm	Wifi	No	
Trains	Bond Street	Credit cards	Yes	
		Alcohol	No	
Buses	113, 189, 2, 274, 30, 74 Orchard Street	W.C.	No	
		Outdoor seating	Yes	
Beans	Workshop	Grinders	Mazzer Robur E x2, Mazzer Major E, Mahlkönig Tanzania	
Machine	Synesso 'Hydra'			
Alternative brewing methods	Aeropress			

Previously working under the name Sensory Lab, this Marylebone outpost of Workshop Coffee Co. was ahead of its time, being one of the first in London to focus on offering a range of filter and brewed coffee at a dedicated brew bar. Aiming to provide more of a one-on-one experience, the brew bar remains prominent in the offering here, as does the consistently high level of coffee served. Akin to Workshop's much larger café in Clerkenwell, where all of the coffee served at both cafés is roasted, the baristas who man the bar are all hugely knowledgeable and implement the company's lofty coffee ambitions with aplomb. The white tiling, grey/green walls and attractive flower arrangements evoke a distinctly Japanese ambiance, and whilst seating is at a premium, the window seats and the bench outside provide perfect vantage points from which to view one of London's more affluent post codes pass by.

West End

FERNANDEZ & WELLS (SOMERSET HOUSE)

Somerset House, Strand WC2R 1LA
Mon-Fri: 8am – 10pm, **Sat:** 10am – 10pm, **Sun:** 10am – 8pm
Trains: Temple
Buses: 1, 168, 171, 172, 188, 243 – Somerset House
www.fernandezandwells.com
@fandwcoffee

NOTES (COVENT GARDEN)

36 Wellington Street WC2E 7BD
Mon-Weds: 8 - 10, **Thurs & Fri:** 8 - 11, **Sat:** 9 - 11, **Sun:** 10 - 6
Trains: Covent Garden
Buses: 11, 13, 139, 15, 176, 23 – Savoy Street
www.notes-uk.co.uk
@NotesCoventGdn

MONMOUTH (COVENT GARDEN)

27 Monmouth Street, Covent Garden WC2H 9EU
Mon- Sat: 8am - 6.30pm
Trains: Covent Garden
Buses: 19, 38 – Cambridge Circus
www.monmouthcoffee.co.uk

MILKBAR

3 Bateman Street, Soho W1D 4AG
Mon- Fri: 8am – 7pm, **Sat & Sun:** 9am – 6pm
Trains: Tottenham Court Road
Buses: 14, 176, 19, 24, 29, 38 – Denmark Street
www.flatwhitecafe.com

FOXCROFT & GINGER

3 Berwick Street, Soho W1F 0DR
Mon: 8am – 7pm, **Tues-Fri:** 8am – 10pm, **Sat:** 9am - 10pm,
Sun: 9am – 7pm
Trains: Leicester Square / Piccadilly Circus
Buses: 19, 38 – Trocadero / Haymarket
www.foxcroftandginger.co.uk
@foxanginger

GINGER & WHITE (SOHO)

1 Silver Place, Soho W1F 0JW
Mon-Fri: 8.30am – 6pm, **Sat:** 10.30am - 6.30pm, **Sun:** Closed
Trains: Piccadilly Circus/Oxford Circus
Buses: 13, 139, 15, 23, 6 – Conduit Street / Hamleys
www.gingerandwhite.com
@gingerandwhite

FERNANDEZ & WELLS (BEAK STREET)

73 Beak Street, Soho W1F 9SR
Mon-Fri: 7.30am – 6pm, **Sat & Sun:** 9am – 6pm
Trains: Goodge Street
Buses: 13, 139, 15, 23, 6 – Conduit Street / Hamleys
www.fernandezandwells.com
@fandwcoffee

NUDE ESPRESSO

19 Soho Square W1D 3QN
Mon-Fri: 8am – 5pm, **Sat & Sun:** 10am – 6pm
Trains: Tottenham Court Road
Buses: 10, 25, 390, 55, 7, 73 – Oxford St / Soho St
www.nudeespresso.com
@NudeEspresso

BEA'S OF BLOOMSBURY

44 Theobalds Road WC1X 8NW
Mon-Fri: 8am – 7pm, **Sat & Sun:** 12pm – 7pm
Trains: Holborn
Buses: 19, 243, 38, 55 – Red Lion Square
www.beasofbloomsbury.com
@beas_bloomsbury

T-A-P COFFEE

26 Rathbone Place, Fitzrovia W1T 1JD
Mon-Fri: 8am – 7pm, **Sat:** 10am – 6pm
Trains: Tottenham Court Road
Buses: 10, 134, 14, 24, 29, 390 – Percy Street
www.tapcoffee.co.uk
@tapcoffee

STORE ST. ESPRESSO

40 Store Street WC1E 7DB
Mon-Fri: 7.30am – 7pm, **Sat:** 10am – 6pm
Trains: Goodge Street
Buses: 10, 134, 24, 29, 390, 73 – Chenies Street
@StoreStEspresso

TAYLOR ST. BARISTAS (MAYFAIR)

22 Brooks Mews, Mayfair W1K 4DY
Mon-Fri: 8am – 5pm
Trains: Bond Street
Buses: 390, 94 – Old Cavendish Street
www.taylor-st.com
@tsb_mayfair

LANTANA

13-14 Charlotte Place, Fitzrovia W1T 1SN
Mon-Fri: 8am – 6pm, **Sat & Sun:** 9am – 5pm
Trains: Goodge Street
Buses: 10, 134, 14, 24, 29, 390 – Goodge Street Station
www.lantanacafe.co.uk
@lantanacafe

THE ATTENDANT

Downstairs, 27a Foley Street W1W 6DY
Mon-Fri: 8am – 6pm, **Sat:** 10am – 5pm
Trains: Oxford Circus / Goodge Street
Buses: 453, 88, C2 – New Cavendish Street
www.the-attendant.com
@AttendantCafe

T-A-P COFFEE

114 Tottenham Court Road W1T 5AH
Mon-Fri: 8am – 7pm, **Sat:** 10am – 6pm
Trains: Warren Street
Buses: 10, 134, 14, 24, 29, 390 – Warren Street Station
www.tapcoffee.co.uk
@tapcoffee

MONOCLE CAFÉ

18 Chiltern Street W1U 7QA
Mon–Fri: 7am – 4pm, **Sat:** 8am – 6pm, **Sun:** 9am – 3pm
Trains: Baker Street / Bond Street
Buses: 113, 2, 274, 30, 74, 82 – Blandford Street
www.monocle.com

FLAT CAP (STRUTTON GROUND)

4 Strutton Ground, Victoria Street SW1P 2HR
Mon–Fri: 8am - 4.30pm
Trains: St James's Park
Buses: 11, 148, 211, 24 – New Scotland Yard
www.notes-uk.co.uk
@FlatCapVictoria

TALKHOUSE COFFEE

275 Portobello Road W11 1LR
Tues-Sat: 8am - 5pm, **Sun:** 10am - 5pm
Trains: Ladbroke Grove
Buses: 7, 70 – Portobello Road
www.talkhousecoffee.com
@TalkhouseCoffee

ELECTRIC COFFEE COMPANY

40 Haven Green, Ealing W5 2NX
Mon–Fri: 7am – 6pm, **Sat:** 8am – 6pm, **Sun:** 9am – 5pm
Trains: Ealing Broadway
Buses: 112, 226, 297, E8 – Ealing Broadway Station
www.electriccoffee.co.uk

East

NUDE ESPRESSO

East

The steady rise of Nude Espresso over the past five years has certainly not gone unnoticed by London's coffee community. Surprisingly, however, it has only recently become apparent that their road to success has become a blueprint for the now swelling wave of café roasteries preparing to launch in 2013. Founders Richard and Gerard started Nude as a café in a Georgian terrace house on Hanbury Street, managing to manoeuvre a small drum roaster into the basement and slowly teaching themselves how to roast. This was in 2008, well before London's coffee culture was something worth writing about, and the pair evidently figured things out as by 2010 the roasting necessitated its own site within the old stables at Brick Lane's Truman Brewery. In 2011, they opened a second café in Soho, further cementing their position in the café scene. By the end of 2012, Nude's roasting operation had fully kicked into gear and word had spread that they were now producing some of the most interesting roasts in the city. Whether or not any of the new breed can replicate Nude's success remains to be seen, but the blueprint is certainly there.

SQUARE MILE
COFFEE ROASTERS

8 Pritchards Road E2 9AP
www.squaremilecoffee.com
@squaremile

By appointment only

No group of people has done more to position London on the global coffee map than the team at Square Mile Coffee Roasters. Founded by former World Barista Champion James Hoffmann and former World Coffee Cup Tasting Champion Anette Moldvaer, Square Mile coffee has consistently been selected by UK baristas for competitions and the company is widely considered to be one of the leading coffee roasters in the world.

Beyond global recognition and awards, Square Mile has influenced and developed London's taste for quality coffee more than any roaster over the past five years. Their seasonal espresso blends and single origin espressos and filter coffees have most often delighted coffee drinkers whilst consistently challenging us to consider new tastes and endlessly reference the flavour wheel. Further underscoring their dedication to greatness, even a recent decaffeinated Yirgacheffe earned praise, causing many to completely reconsider decaf coffee. It's fair to say that the level of quality that Square Mile has come to represent has become a benchmark for food producers across the capital and roasters around the world.

Square Mile beans are found in a number of London's best coffee shops and their packaging has become a sign of distinction. Their trademark Red Brick espresso is a seasonal blend that is continually tweaked. The blends showcase what they consider to be the best beans currently available and has generally been comprised of three beans. At times these beans have been available individually as well, alongside a variety of other carefully sourced coffees from around the world. The previous year has seen a strong showing from Ethiopia with the fruity natural processed Jirmiwachu appearing as both an espresso and a filter, alongside the ever popular Wote Yirgacheffe.

The past year also saw the return of Square Mile's Sweet Shop espresso. Now offered permanently alongside the Red Brick blend, the latest incarnation of Sweet Shop, combining an equal percentage of Musasa from Rwanda and Deri Kochi from Ethiopia, is incredibly fruity and far more complex than the great majority of espressos available. Those with a taste for fruity coffee will be pleased to know that the roasters' goal with these blends is to cram "as much fruit into the cup as possible". Like Red Brick, this blend will change regularly, but it provides more of an opportunity for the Square Mile team to be expressive and experimental.

The team at Square Mile roast on a hulking 1950s cast iron Menado Superior in the back of their discreet headquarters on a side street in East London. Neither the roastery's name or griffin logo adorn the building in which some of the world's highest quality coffee beans inspire some of the world's finest roasters. But keep an eye out for a little white van. This means something delicious is ready for delivery across London.

CLIMPSON & SONS

Arch 374, Helmsley Place
E8 3SB
www.climsonandsons.com
@climpsonandsons / @climpsonsarch

Thurs & Fri: 5pm - 11pm
Sat: 1pm - 12am
Sun: 1pm - 10.30pm

When walking into the arches that house Climpson & Sons' latest East London hideout, it's hard not to feel that they're living the dream. Not only is the space beautiful - the perfect combination of low-slung atmospherics and ad hoc construction - but pairing a coffee roaster and a craft beer brewery bar under the same roof is about as good as it gets, in our humble opinion.

Alongside providing a space to roast Climpson & Sons' espresso blends and single origin coffees, both for their wholesale clients and the original café through the park on Broadway Market, the arches are also a fully licensed, multi-purpose events space. The beer side of the equation comes by way of London Field's Brewery, which is part-owned by Ian Burgess, founder of Climpson & Sons. In addition, come the fairer months, the outside area hosts a barbeque from Thursday to Sunday, just in case you had ideas about ever leaving. Great beer, tasty BBQ and fine coffee - what more could anyone want?

46B ESPRESSO HUT

46b Brooksby's Walk E9 6DA
www. 46b-espressohut.tumblr.com
@46b_ espressohut

East

Hours	Mon-Fri: 7.30am-6.30pm Sat: 9am-6.30pm Sun: 10am-6.30pm	Wifi	Yes
		Credit cards	No
		Alcohol	No
Trains	Homerton	W.C.	Yes
Buses	236, 242, 276, 308, 425 Brooksby's Walk	Outdoor seating	Yes

Beans	Square Mile	Grinders	Anfim Super Caimano
Machine	Synesso 'Cyncra'		
Alternative brewing methods	Technivorm Moccamaster		

Despite the substantial growth of quality cafés in 2012, the number of excellent neighbourhood coffee shops outside central London can still be counted on one hand. Amongst these is Homerton's 46b Espresso Hut, which deserves considerable praise for both the quality of the coffee and the distinctive atmosphere. Owners Eva and Dom bring a thoughtful approach to the café, situated on the ground floor of a quaint 18th century townhouse that has previously been used for such diverse purposes as a chocolate factory and a motorcycle garage. The idiosyncrasies of the space are evidently in safe hands and the local community has embraced it. The coffee is served by Eva who expertly handles Square Mile beans on the Synesso, with filter coffee available in the mornings. Dom produces an original menu of delicious sandwiches on bread from E5 Bakehouse, making use of the wide range of quality produce in the area. It's fair to say that more than any other coffee shop opening in 2012, this cosy café has captured the heart of London's coffee community.

UNION
HAND ROASTED

7a South Crescent
E16 4TL
www.unionroasted.com
@unionroasted

By appointment only

Conversations during a cupping with Union's co-founder Steven Macatonia may begin with aromas and taste but they inevitably lead to the stories about the origin farms, their owners and very often the farmers themselves. Coffee at Union is clearly recognised as part of a bigger picture. Indeed, it would be difficult to find a roastery more dedicated to ensuring an ethical approach to sourcing coffee and supporting sustainable coffee-driven communities than Union.

Union holds a unique position amongst speciality coffee roasters in London with its direct trade relationships - approximately 90% of their coffee is direct trade - and its capacity to straddle the divide between fiercely independent cafés and supermarkets. Their most recently acquired client, Harris & Hoole - a new quality-driven chain led by the founders of Taylor Street Baristas - will lead to a significant increase in production. This growth, Macatonia explains, allows for new sourcing opportunities and further direct trade relationships with farms. Proof that at Union, every conversation leads back to origin.

TAYLOR ST. BARISTAS
SOUTH QUAY

1 Harbour Exchange Square, South Quay E14 9GE
www.taylor-st.com
@TSB_South_Quay

East

Hours	Mon-Fri: 8am - 5pm	Wifi	Yes
Trains	South Quay DLR	Credit cards	Yes
Buses	D3, D6, D8 Harbour Exchange Square	Alcohol	No
		W.C.	Yes
		Outdoor seating	Yes

Beans	Union Hand Roasted, Square Mile	Grinders	Mazzer Robur E, Nuova Simonelli Mythos, Mahlkönig Tanzania
Machine	Nuova Simonelli 'Aurelia' T3, Bunn ICB Batch Brewer		

Alternative brewing methods Clever Dripper

South Quay may not be the most obvious leisure destination for most coffee tourists but the large number of office buildings and skyscrapers that now tower over this area of London necessitate a café every bit as decent as its surrounds. Having kept most of the city's financial district caffeine fuelled for the past half decade, Taylor St. Baristas is the obvious outfit to supply South Quay's steady demand for great coffee. The space is bright and open - this being the largest of TSB's cafés - and always houses enough coffee options, sandwiches and sweets to get you through even the most tiresome of work days. If you're simply here for pleasure then venturing to South Quay is highly recommended, if not to sample another in the growing line of fine Taylor St. outlets then to appreciate how much the London skyline has changed in recent years.

OTHER EAST SPECIALITY COFFEE LOCATIONS

ALLPRESS ESPRESSO

58 Redchurch Street, Shoreditch E2 7DP
Mon-Fri: 8am - 5pm, **Sat & Sun:** 9am – 5pm
Trains: Shoreditch High Street
Buses: 388, 8 - Shoreditch High Street Station
www.allpressespresso.com
@AllpressE2

LEILA'S SHOP

15-17 Calvert Avenue, Bethnal Green E2 7JP
Mon & Tues: Closed, **Weds-Sat:** 10am – 6pm, **Sun:** 10am – 5pm
Trains: Shoreditch High Street
Buses: 149, 242, 26, 35, 47, 48 – Shoreditch High Street Station
www.vegboxers.com
@Leilas_Shop

FULL STOP

202 Brick Lane E1 6SA
Mon & Tues: 7.30am - 9.30pm, **Wed & Thurs:** 7.30am - 11pm,
Fri: 7.30am -12.30am, **Sat:** 9am - 12.30am, **Sun:** 9am - 9.30pm
Trains: Shoreditch High Street
Buses: 388, 8 – Brick Lane
@fullstopbar

MERITO COFFEE

Broadway Market E8
Sat: 8.30am – 4pm
Trains: London Fields / Cambridge Heath
Buses: 236, 394 – Broadway Market
www.meritocoffee.com
@MeritoCoffee

HACKNEY BUREAU

3 Mare Street E8 4RP
Mon-Fri: 7am – 6pm, **Sat & Sun:** 9am – 6pm
Trains: Cambridge Heath
Buses: 106, 254, 26, 388, 48, 55 – Mare Street
www.hackneybureau.com
@HACKNEY_BUREAU

TERRONE (NETIL MARKET)

11-25 Westgate Street, Hackney E8
Sat: 9.30am – 6pm
Trains: London Fields
Buses: 106, 254, 26, 388, 48, D6 – St. Joseph's Hospice
www.terrone.co.uk
@Terrone

PAVILION

Crown Gate West, Victoria Park London E9 7DE
Summer: Mon-Fri: 8am – 4.30pm, **Sat & Sun:** 8am – 5pm
Winter: Mon-Sun: 8am – 4pm
Trains: Mile End / Bethnal Green
Buses: 277, 425 – Victoria Park
www.the-pavilion-cafe.com
@pavilionvicpark

REILLY ROCKET

507 Kingsland Road, Dalston E8 4AU
Mon-Fri: 7.30am - 5pm, **Sat:** 9am - 5pm, **Sun:** 10am - 5pm
Trains: Dalston Junction
Buses: 149, 242, 243, 488, 67, 76 – Kingsland Rd / Forest Rd
www.reillyrocket.com
@reillyrocket

WILTON WAY CAFÉ

63 Wilton Way E8 1BG
Mon-Fri: 8am - 5pm, **Sat:** 8am – 6pm, **Sun:** 9am – 6pm
Trains: Hackney Downs / Hackney Central
Buses: 242, 277, 38 – Royal Oak Road
www.londonfieldsradio.com
@WiltonWayCafe

RAILROAD

120-122 Morning Lane, Hackney E9 6LH
Mon & Tues: Closed, **Wed-Sat:** 11am – 11pm, **Sun:** 10am – 5pm
Trains: Homerton / Hackney Central
Buses: 236, 276, 30, W15 – Homerton Terrace
www.railroadhackney.co.uk
@Railroadhackney

MOUSE & DE LOTZ

103 Shacklewell Lane E8 2EB
Mon-Fri: 8am – 6pm, **Sat:** 9am – 6pm, **Sun:** 10am – 6pm
Trains: Dalston Kingsland / Hackney Downs
Buses: 149, 243, 67, 76 – Princess May Road
www.mousedelotz.com

BLACK & WHITE COFFEE CO.

Chatsworth Road Market,
Chatsworth Road E5 0LH
Sun: 10am – 3pm
Trains: Clapton
Buses: 242, 308 – Chatsworth Road
www.blackandwhitecoffee.co.uk

BLACK & WHITE COFFEE CO.

Outside the Palm 2 Store,
151–152 Lower Clapton Road E5 0QJ
Sat: 7am – 3pm, **Sun:** 8am – 3pm
Trains: Clapton
Buses: 106, 253, 38, 425, 48, 488 – Clapton Pond
www.blackandwhitecoffee.co.uk

THE COUNTER CAFÉ

7 Roach Road E3 2PA
Mon-Fri: 8am – 5pm, **Sat & Sun:** 9am – 5pm
Trains: Hackney Wick / Pudding Mill Lane
Buses: 276, 488 – Wansbeck Road
www.thecountercafe.co.uk
@thecountercafe

HACKNEY PEARL

11 Prince Edward Road, Hackney Wick E9 5LX
Mon-Fri: 8am – 11pm, **Sat & Sun:** 10am – 11pm
Trains: Hackney Wick
Buses: 26, 388, 488 – Hackney Wick / Trowbridge Road
www.thehackneypearl.com
@thehackneypearl

GRIND COFFEE BAR (WESTFIELD)

5C The Great Eastern Market, Westfield Shopping Centre, Stratford City E20 1EH
Mon- Fri: 8am – 9pm, **Sat:** 9am – 9pm, **Sun:** 11am – 6pm
Trains: Stratford
Buses: 11, 13, 139, 15, 176, 23 – Savoy Street
www.grindcoffeebar.co.uk
@GrindCoffeeBar

TAYLOR ST. BARISTAS (CANARY WHARF)

8 South Colonnade, Canary Wharf E14 4PZ
Mon-Fri: 7am – 6pm
Trains: Canary Wharf
Buses: 135, 277, D3, D7, D8 – Canada Square South
www.taylor-st.com
@TSBCanaryWharf

EMBASSY EAST

285 Hoxton Street N1 5JX
www.embassyeast.co.uk
@EmbassyEast

Hours	Mon-Fri: 8 - 6pm	Wifi	Yes
	Sat & Sun: 10am - 6pm	Credit cards	Yes
Trains	Hoxton / Haggerston	Alcohol	No
Buses	67, 243, 394, 149	W.C.	Yes
	Hoxton Street Market	Outdoor seating	Yes

Beans	Workshop	Grinders	Anfim Super Caimano, Mahlkönig Columbia
Machine	La Marzocco 'Linea'		
Alternative brewing methods	Chemex, French press		

Having met one another working behind the espresso machine at Soho institution Flat White, friends Lehi, Chris and Tommy slowly forged their plans to open a coffee shop of their own. Drawing on all their experience as baristas in one of the capital's most renowned coffee shops, with Embassy East the able trio have created a standard and an atmosphere that certainly rivals their previous employers, though with a distinctly East London edge. The owners' charm and the quality of service they offer comes as no surprise, as does the interior, with its school benches (complete with original compass carvings), open plan kitchen and the on-trend design elements that are all nicely indicative of this part of town. But where Embassy East really delivers is the no-nonsense, stripped back coffee menu - consisting 4, 6 or 8oz cups of black, white or filter coffee - and an array of quality, wholesome food offerings, such as breakfasts, open sandwiches and soups. It all works together with a kind of joyous simplicity. And simplicity, as those who have tried will attest, is the hardest thing to get right.

TINA, WE SALUTE YOU

47 King Henry's Walk, Islington N1 4NH
www.tinawesaluteyou.com
@tinawesaluteyou

North

Hours	Mon-Fri: 8am - 6pm Sat & Sun: 10am - 7pm	Wifi	Yes
		Credit cards	No
Trains	Dalston Kingsland	Alcohol	No
Buses	67, 76, 149, 243, 488 Dalston Kingsland Station	W.C.	Yes
		Outdoor seating	Yes
Beans	Square Mile	Grinders	Anfim Super Caimano
Machine	La Marzocco 'Linea'		

London has only a handful of truly excellent neighbourhood cafés and it would be impossible to list them without including Dalston's somewhat legendary Tina, We Salute You. Tina's - as the owners Danny and Steve call it - serves first rate coffee using Square Mile alongside a simple yet delicious menu of homemade breakfast and lunch.

Beyond the quality coffee and food, Tina's boasts truly interesting art, a loyalty wall of epic proportions and what is without a doubt the most attractive clientele in London. The art - showcasing work by local artists - rotates every few months and is overlooked by J.H. Lynch's 1960s portrait of Tina; a monument to sultriness if there ever was one. After four years in business, the loyalty wall - on which customers scribble their names and tally up their coffees - is likely closing in on listed status. But Tina's will always have space for new regulars and more names on the wall so if you haven't visited yet, make sure you do.

CARAVAN
KING'S CROSS

Granary Building, 1 Granary Square NC1 4AA
www.caravankingscross.co.uk
@CaravanKingsX

North

Hours	Mon-Tues: 8am - 10.30pm Weds & Thurs: 8am - 11pm Fri: 8am - 12am Sat: 10am - 12am Sun: 10am - 4pm	Buses	10, 17, 259, 390, 59, 91 Wharfdale Road
		Wifi	Yes
		Credit cards	Yes
		Alcohol	Yes
Trains	King's Cross	W.C.	Yes
		Outdoor seating	No

Beans	Caravan	Grinders	Mazzer Robur E x5, Mahlkönig Tanzania
Machines	La Marzocco 'Strada', La Marzocco 'Linea' x 2		

Alternative brewing methods V60, Aeropress, Woodneck

I f there were to be a space that best represented the meteoric rise of the multi-purpose café in London, then Caravan King's Cross is most probably it. Several years ago, such a place would have been a stand alone in the capital; a behemoth more at home on the streets of Melbourne or Sydney. Such is the changing face of coffee in the UK, Caravan has slid in as though it were always there, and provides a coffee and food menu as influenced by Antipodean café culture as it is by London's own growing gastronomic identity.

The café itself is beautifully integrated into its impressive surrounds with industrial detailing that references the heritage of the site, being that this is a grade II listed Victorian granary building. This area of the city used to be a district notorious for some of London's less salubrious nightlife but which has undergone a multi-billion pound redevelopment plan in recent years and now goes under its new moniker, King's Cross Central. The shoots of this regeneration are already very much visible and Caravan King's Cross is one of the first to make this neighbourhood a home.

Having found your way across the expanse of courtyard - largely frequented by bright young things from Central St. Martin's Art College next door - you are greeted by one of the most appealing café restaurant spaces in London and one of the very few where the standards and dedication to food are matched by the coffee on offer. Caravan's founders, Miles Kirby and Chris Ammerman, began their exploration of roasting coffee in the basement of their first café - Caravan Exmouth Market - two years ago. Since then they have seemingly mastered the process, gaining an impressive wholesale client list along the way. Unlike the cramped confines of the Exmouth Market basement, the new space at King's Cross allows ample room to roast, cup and sample coffees in a custom training area, situated beside the drum of their giant Probat roaster.

Whilst all manner of coffee gadgetry adorns the countertops and the baristas - some of whom you'll recognise from other speciality coffee shops around the city - ensure that everyone is catered for in that department, it is also the food offering that makes Caravan King's Cross representative of London's current breed of café restaurants. Influences and ingredients from around the world infuse the menu with both familiar and exotic small plates and dishes, and the warehouse-sized, canteen-style dining area becomes alive during busy service periods, with friendly floor staff flowing between tables and chefs working skilfully, only partly obscured from full view by the wire divides that separate the kitchen and restaurant area. With great coffee, an exciting menu and a first-rate location, Caravan King's Cross certainly seems to have all the bases covered.

THE FIELDS BENEATH

52a Prince of Wales Road NW5 3LN
@FieldsBeneath

North

Hours	Mon-Fri: 7.30am - 5pm Sat: 9am - 2pm	Wifi	Yes
		Credit cards	Yes
Trains	Kentish Town West / Kentish Town	Alcohol	No
Buses	393, 46, 24, 134 Kentish Town West Station	W.C.	No
		Outdoor seating	Yes
Beans	Round Hill, Federation, Butterworth & Son, Square Mile	Machine	La Marzocco 'Linea'
		Grinders	Anfim Barista

We first stumbled upon this little gem quite literally when making our mazy way from the Camden Town Brewery bar round the corner, a discovery which provided much intrigue when we spied a La Marzocco on the Morrocan tiled bar top and Square Mile retail bags on the shelves. Furthermore, when we returned during daylight hours, we were more than pleasantly surprised by everything The Fields Beneath had to offer.

Co-owner Gavin Fernback previously ran a popular coffee cart near Chalk Farm Tube, where he fortuitously met Sibylle Meyfret and with whom he opened The Fields Beneath under the arches in late 2012. As any good independent should be, they are dedicated to proper, honest sourcing of all their goods, not least the coffee they serve – provided by a host of the UK's best up-and-coming roasters. This sourcing policy extends to all of their goods, from milk to juice to pastries, so expect only the finest ingredients. And if you're curious about the name, see the stack of books by Gillian Tindall on the shelf; as much of a loving ode to Kentish Town as the café itself.

VAGABOND N4

Unit 20, Stroud Green Road N4 3SG
@VagabondN4

Hours	Mon-Sun: 7am - 7pm	Wifi	Yes
Trains	Crouch Hill	Credit cards	Yes
Buses	210, W3, W7 Tollington Park	Alcohol	No
		W.C.	Yes
		Outdoor seating	Yes
Beans	Has Bean	Grinders	Mazzer Super Jolly, Mahlkönig K30
Machine	Nuova Simonelli 'Aurelia 2'		

North

A former barista at Tapped & Packed, Dainius set up Vagabond on an unlikely corner of Finsbury Park in 2012. Within this once desolate coffee landscape, the café is thriving and the local community's support is unprecedented. Along with his nephew Povilas and a team of talented baristas and chefs, Dainius has created what is without a doubt the beginning of a serious North London coffee business.

Vagabond N4 has a raw appearance - built using second hand scaffolding boards and incorporating familiar rough coffee sacks. This style has been expanded upon in their new, and by all respects huge café on Holloway Road - Vagabond N7 - which also integrates a considerable selection of second hand materials.

Both coffee shops serve espressos from Has Bean - with the Blake blend available at Vagabond N4 - and offer guest filters daily. Spearheaded by the quality exemplified by Vagabond's baristas, the north London coffee scene is set to take off.

COFFEEWORKS PROJECT
96-98 Islington High Street N1 8EG
Mon-Fri: 7.30am – 6pm, **Sat:** 9am – 6pm, **Sun:** 10am – 4pm
Trains: Angel
Buses: 19, 30, 4, 43 – Angel Station
www.coffeeworksproject.com
@CoffeeWorksProj

GIDDY UP (ANGEL)
Islington Green N1 8DU
Mon-Fri: 8am – 2.30pm, **Sat & Sun:** 10am – 4pm
Trains: Angel
Buses: 341, 38, 476, 56, 73 – Islington Green
www.giddyupcoffee.co.uk
@GiddyUpAngel

MAISON D'ETRE
154 Canonbury Road, Highbury & Islington N1 2UP
Mon-Fri: 7.30am – 6pm, **Sat & Sun:** 9am – 6pm
Trains: Highbury & Islington
Buses: 19, 277, 393, 4 – Highbury Corner
www.maisondetrecafe.co.uk
@maisondetrecafe

VAGABOND N7

105 Holloway Road N7 8LT
Mon-Fri: 7am – 8pm, **Sat & Sun:** 9am – 8pm
Trains: Highbury & Islington
Buses: 271, 393, 43 – St Mary Magdalene Church
@VagabondN7

NOTES AT TILEYARD

6a Tileyard Studios N7 9AH
Mon-Fri: 7.30am – 5.30pm
Trains: Caledonian Road & Barnsbury
Buses: 274, 390 – Brewery Road
www.notes-uk.co.uk
@NotesTileyard

LEYAS

20 Camden High Street NW1 0JH
Mon-Fri: 7.30am – 6pm, **Sat & Sun:** 9am – 5.30pm
Trains: Mornington Crescent
Buses: 27, 88 – Mornington Crescent Station
www.leyas.co.uk
@leyascoffee

FRED & FRAN

55 Kynaston Road, Stoke Newington N16 0EB
Mon-Fri: 8.30am – 5pm, **Sat:** 9am – 5pm, **Sun:** 10am – 4pm
Trains: Rectory Road
Buses: 393, 476, 73 – Bouverie Road
www.fredandfran.com
@fredandfrann16

GINGER & WHITE (BELSIZE PARK)

2 England's Lane NW3 4TG
Mon-Fri: 7.30am - 5.30pm, **Sat & Sun:** 8.30am - 5.30pm
Trains: Belsize Park
Buses: 168, **C11 – Upper Park Road**
www.gingerandwhite.com
@gingerandwhite

MERITO COFFEE

Eton Avenue, Swiss Cottage NW3
Wednesday & Friday: 8.30am – 3pm
Trains: Swiss Cottage
Buses: 113, 13, 187, 268, 31, 82, C11
Swiss Cottage Station
www.meritocoffee.com
@MeritoCoffee

GINGER & WHITE (HAMPSTEAD)

4a-5a Perrin's Court NW3 1QS
Mon-Fri: 7.30am - 5.30pm, **Sat & Sun:** 8.30am - 5.30pm
Trains: Hampstead
Buses: 268, 46 – Hampstead Station / Hampstead High Street
www.gingerandwhite.com
@gingerandwhite

COFFEE CIRCUS

136 Crouch Hill, Crouch End N8 9DX
Mon-Fri: 8am – 6pm, **Sat & Sun:** 9am – 6pm
Trains: Highgate / Harringay
Buses: 41, 91, W7 – Edison Road
www.coffeecircus.com
@CoffeeCircusLtd

CRAFT COFFEE

The Ropewalk, Maltby Street Market SE1 3PA
www.craft-coffee.co.uk
@Craft_Coffee

South

| Hours | Sat: 9am - 3pm | Buses | 188, 343, 381, 47 Tanner Street |
| Trains | Bermondsey | | |

Beans	Has Bean	Grinders	Mazzer Robur E, Mahlkönig Tanzania
Machine	Nuova Simonelli 'Appia'		
Alternative brewing methods	Technivorm Moccamaster		

Despite its relatively small scale, Maltby Street Market is home to the finest independent quality food and drink producers in London. This remarkable foodie stretch begins with Monmouth Coffee's well-established roastery and continues in an ad hoc manner before spilling into Druid Street Market - home to the excellent Coleman Coffee and others. A new-comer along the so-called Ropewalk is an attractively built coffee cart situated outside Bea's Diner called Craft Coffee.

Run by partners Emily and Jamie, both former baristas at Bea's of Bloomsbury, Craft Coffee rotates single origin espressos and filters from Has Bean every Saturday when the market opens for business. Despite numerous quality coffee options nearby, Craft Coffee has quickly found its niche and a loyal clientele. Offering single origin coffee three ways - as espresso, espresso and milk and filter - Emily and Jamie thrive serving London's most discerning foodies, so much so that plans for an additional cart are underway. The cart, which they wheel out of Bea's arch every Saturday, was built by Jamie's father who has committed to building two more, making a promising future look certain.

MONMOUTH
DOCKLEY ROAD

Arch 3, Spa North
(between Dockley Rd and Spa Road) SE16 4RP
www.monmouthcoffee.co.uk

Hours	Sat: 8am - 12pm	Wifi	No
Trains	Bermondsey	Credit cards	No
Buses	188, 381, 47, C10 St James's Road	Alcohol	No
		W.C.	No
		Outdoor seating	No

Beans	Monmouth	Grinders	Mazzer Robur E, Ditting
Machine	La Marzocco 'Linea'		
Alternative brewing methods	Filter Cone		

South

We're always keen to champion the more hidden coffee destinations, and they don't come smaller or more hard to find than the newest of Monmouth's three locations. Housed underneath the railway arches in Bermondsey, this may not be the place to sit and while away hours over several rounds of coffee and there is no food on offer, but this cute little archway selling retail bags and takeaway drinks has an enormous amount going for it. Most notably, this area is being transformed by a score of independent businesses, largely specialising in premium, handmade food and drinks, who are working with Southwark Council to restore this neighbourhood to its former foodie glory. This means that on Saturdays you'll find a hive of activity, from the jovial atmosphere at the Kernel Brewery, to people buying loaves from the Little Bread Pedlar and queues winding from the doorway of The Ham & Cheese Co. Discover it - and Monmouth's latest incarnation - before all your friends do.

DARK FLUID

Brockley Market, Lewisham Way SE4 1UT
www.darkfluid.co.uk
@DarkFluidCoffee

Hours	Sat: 10am – 2pm	**Buses**	136, 21, 321, 436 Lewisham College
Trains	St John's		

Beans	Dark Fluid	**Grinder**	Mazzer Major
Machine	Izzo 'Pompei'		
Alternative brewing methods	Technivorm Moccamaster		

South

Anchoring the popular Brockley Market every Saturday morning, Lawrence Sinclair and his crew behind the lever machine are familiar to coffee connoisseurs and foodies across the capital. But for many south of the river, Dark Fluid remains a closely kept secret despite its quiet ascent into the upper echelons of UK coffee roasters. Becoming south east London's roaster of choice has clearly benefited us all and Dark Fluid continues to raise standards as well as eyebrows.

Some will remember Lawrence, the founder and leading roaster at Dark Fluid, from his days running the Exchange Coffee stall in Lewisham Market. A seemingly incongruous setting for top notch coffee if there ever was one, Lawrence was steadfast and evidently born to introduce the area to his superior product. In fact, Lawrence identifies the genesis of Dark Fluid to a "mad day of open air roasting" in the market. Today, the Dark Fluid team roasts in a more suitable yet equally original setting and sources to a slew of local cafés and restaurants, not to mention UK-wide clients as far as Sheffield and the Welsh borders.

Popular London spots to try Dark Fluid beyond Brockley Market include the lovely With Jam and Bread in Lee, the incredibly welcoming The Dish & the Spoon in Nunhead, the hip and high quality Arlo & Moe in Crofton Park and the delicious Hand Made Food in Blackheath. It's a testament to Dark Fluid's strong reputation that none of these cafés looked further than their local roaster when setting up shop. Dark Fluid beans can also be seen as an occasional guest offering at places like Notes in Covent Garden.

As a former chef, Lawrence has a highly trained palette - as you would expect from a roaster - but equally he has a keen understanding of his customers' tastes. His Brockley Market stall is critical in that he is one of the few London roasters who has direct contact with - and regular feedback from - his customers. This suits Lawrence well as he is constantly experimenting with and improving his roasts.

Dark Fluid's signature espresso blend, Schrödinger's Cat, is tweaked throughout the year, but its primary component is always Malacara. Grown in the nutrient-rich soil surrounding the Santa Ana volcano in El Salvador's "golden coffee belt", the Malacara is a fruity well-balanced coffee which Lawrence compliments with other high quality beans. As a boutique roaster, Dark Fluid isn't forced to meet massive volume demands and ensures that he selects the finest green beans available at any given time.

While Dark Fluid enjoys success and recognition across the country, it is south east London that has benefitted most. As the speciality coffee industry quickly spreads throughout the area, more and more people will either find themselves considering the mysteries of quantum physics or, like me, simply queueing up at Brockley Market for another Schrödinger's Cat espresso.

BROWNS OF BROCKLEY

5 Coulgate Street SE4 2RW
www.brownsofbrockley.com
@brownsofse4

South

Hours	Mon-Fri: 7.30am - 6pm	Wifi	Yes
	Sat: 9am - 5pm	Credit cards	Yes
	Sun: 10am - 4pm		
Trains	Brockley	Alcohol	No
Buses	171, 172, 484	W.C.	Yes
	Brockley Station	Outdoor seating	No

Beans	Square Mile	Grinders	Mazzer Robur E x2
Machine	La Marzocco 'Strada'		
Alternative brewing methods	V60		

Situated directly across from the Overground Station, Browns is as good an entry point into Brockley as you will find. The café reflects the increasingly popular neighbourhood's character with its friendly approach and high standards without forced pretensions. Serving beans roasted by Square Mile, the staff are as enthusiastic about coffee as they are skilled. Filter is available daily - cold brewed and served on ice during the summer months - and the espresso-based drinks are carefully prepared and delivered. Browns also offers a variety of excellent sandwiches, cakes and pastries which are all produced in-house. The window display of these fresh baked goods along with consistently lovely flower arrangements make the café a welcoming sight and a difficult spot to pass without popping in. It is no wonder that a variety of newly opened cafés nearby point to Browns as their inspiration for opening and aspiration for quality. For those looking for a cosy neighbourhood café to chat or unwind in beyond the bustle of London, Browns of Brockley is your sanctuary.

FEDERATION

Unit 77-78, Brixton Village Market SW9 8PS
www.federationcoffee.com
@FederationCoffe

Hours	Mon-Weds: 8am - 5pm Thurs & Fri: 8am - 6pm Sat: 9am - 6pm Sun: 9am - 5pm	Wifi	Yes
		Credit cards	Yes
		Alcohol	No
Trains	Brixton	W.C.	No
Buses	322, 3, 35, 355, 59, 2 Brixton Station	Outdoor seating	N/A
Beans	Federation, Nude	Grinders	Mazzer Robur E, Anfim Super Caimano
Machine	Synesso 'Cyncra'		

Whether down to luck or a keen sense of intuition, the choice to set up a coffee shop under the run-down archways of Brixton Village Market in 2010 has turned out to be one of the best decisions Nick Coates and George Wallace ever made. The pair decided to give up their careers in London's financial sector to follow their dream of working in coffee; a bold move when considering both the economic climate and the fact that Londoner's were not so admiring of great coffee as they were in the duo's homeland of New Zealand. In honesty, there was no decent coffee for miles around, less still a café culture to speak of. Back then the village market, which had once been one of Brixton's cultural landmarks, had also seen better days and the shops that did still operate there were unable to draw the crowds they used to. But in the couple of years since, Federation has helped change the face of Market Row and itself blossomed into one of the must-visit destinations in Brixton.

Whilst part of their success lies in the café's location, the fact that they continue to serve consistently flawless coffees certainly helps. Their recently established roastery nearby, where Nick now hand roasts all of Federation's coffee, means that the house espresso is their very own Contraband blend, consisting 50% Brazilian pulped natural and 50% Ethiopia natural. This new addition provides the basis for all their coffee drinks and is sold retail alongside a host of home coffee brewing equipment and hand grinders, so that you can also enjoy their coffee in the comfort of your own home. It's also the mainstay in the hopper at the second Federation Coffee outlet on Brighton Terrace. Whilst much smaller than the original café, Federation 2.0 is ideal for a quick takeaway and benefits from a cluster of outdoor seating during the warmer months.

Since Federation opened it has proved somewhat of a catalyst for other artisan food producers, who have since made home under the arches and renewed the buzz that had been lacking for some time. Now the market has its swagger back, not to mention a host of independent eateries, including Franco Manca, perhaps the neighbourhood's best pizzeria, and Honest Burgers, one of London's hip new breed of burger restaurants that practically redefines the genre. But when it comes to coffee, the title of 'Best Coffee in Brixton', which adorns the A-board outside the café, may have a growing number of worthy pretenders in south London, but remains an accolade that still rightly belongs to Federation.

BIRDHOUSE

123 St. John's Hill, Battersea SW11 1SZ
www.birdhou.se
@BirdhouseUK

Hours	Mon-Fri: 7am - 4pm Sat & Sun: 9am - 5pm	Wifi	No
Trains	Clapham Junction	Credit cards	Yes
Buses	156, 170, 337, 37, 39 87, 639, 670 Brussels Road	Alcohol	No
		W.C.	Yes
		Outdoor seating	Yes

South

Beans	Climpson & Sons	Grinder	Anfim Super Caimano
Machine	La Marzocco 'Linea'		

Birdhouse is owned and operated by Cameron and Alexei, two former graphic designers from Melbourne, who have utilised their collective eye for detail to create a café space laden with satisfying design features. The battered work bench that serves as a countertop, matched with the slate grey walls and yellow detailing strike a beautiful, understated chord. It's impossible not to relate the look and feel of Birdhouse with the abundance of fine cafés to be found in the duo's home city, which is a satisfying anomaly given that it's not situated 10,000 miles away, but just a short stroll up St. John's Hill away from Clapham High Street. As you would expect from the Aussie café comparison, the coffee at Birdhouse is one of its major selling points, especially given that the café is in particularly sparse coffee territory. Their espresso, roasted by Climpson & Sons in East London, is unsurprisingly the best for several miles around and their sumptuous selection of sandwiches, such as the highly recommended 'Special' chicken BLT, also fill the void previously found in this particular London postcode.

South

OTHER SOUTH SPECIALITY COFFEE LOCATIONS

MONMOUTH (BOROUGH MARKET)
2 Park Street, The Borough SE1 9AB
Mon-Sat: 7.30am – 6pm
Trains: London Bridge
Buses: 343, 381, 47 – Hay's Galleria
www.monmouthcoffee.co.uk

NATIONAL THEATRE ESPRESSO BAR
Theatre Square, Upper Ground, South Bank SE1 9PX
Mon-Sat: 9am - 7.30pm, **Sun:** 12pm – 5pm
Trains: Waterloo
Buses: 1, 139, 168, 171, 172, RV1 – Waterloo Bridge / South Bank
www.nationaltheatre.org.uk

COLEMAN COFFEE
Unit 5, Dockley Estate, Dockley Road SE16 3SN
Saturday: 8.30am – 3pm
Trains: Bermondsey
Buses: 188, 381, 47, C10 – Bermondsey Station
www.colemancoffee.com
@ColemanCoffee

FEDERATION COFFEE 2.0

9 Brighton Terrace, Brixton SW9 8DJ
Mon-Fri: 8am – 4pm
Trains: Brixton
Buses: 196, 2, 250, 333, 35, 45 – Brixton Station
www.federationcoffee.com
@FederationCoffe

GRIND COFFEE BAR (BATTERSEA)

1 Windward House, Plantation Wharf SW11 3TY
Mon-Fri: 7.30am – 4pm
Trains: Clapham Junction
Buses: 295, 44, C3 – Hope Street
www.grindcoffeebar.co.uk
@GrindCoffeeBar

VOLCANO COFFEE HOUSE

Unit F01, Parkhall Trading Estate, 40 Martell Rd SE21 8EN
Mon-Fri: 8am - 4.30pm, **Sat:** 10am – 4pm
Trains: West Dulwich
Buses: 322 – Martell Road
www.volcanocoffeeworks.com
@Volcano_Coffee

WITH JAM & BREAD

386 Lee High Road, Lee Green SE12 8RW
Mon-Fri: 8am - 4.30pm, **Sat:** 9.30am – 4pm,
Sun: 9.30am - 3.30pm
Trains: Blackheath / Lee
Buses: 122, 178, 261, 321, 621 – Lampmead Road
www.withjamandbread.com
@WithJamandBread

BAMBINO COFFEE

32 Church Road, Crystal Palace SE19 2ET
Thurs & Fri: 11am – 5pm, **Sat & Sun:** 10am – 5pm
Trains: Crystal Palace
Buses: 249, 322, 417, 432, 450 – Westow Hill
www.bambinocoffee.wordpress.com
@BambinoCoffee

M1LK

20 Bedford Hill, Balham SW12 9RG
Mon-Sat: 8am – 5pm, **Sun:** 9am – 5pm
Trains: Balham
Buses: 155, 249, 315, 355 – Hildreth Street Market
www.m1lk.co.uk
@m1lkcoffee

GRIND COFFEE BAR (PUTNEY)

79 Lower Richmond Road SW15 2ET
Mon-Fri: 7am – 5pm, **Sat & Sun:** 8.30am – 5pm
Trains: Putney Bridge
Buses: 22, 265, 485 – Ruvigny Gardens
www.grindcoffeebar.co.uk
@GrindCoffeeBar

TRIED & TRUE

279 Upper Richmond Road SW15 6SP
Mon-Fri: 7.30am – 4pm, **Sat & Sun:** 8.30am - 4.30pm
Trains: Putney
Buses: 337, 430 – Putney Leisure Centre
www.triedandtruecafe.co.uk
@tried_true_cafe

Coffee
Compendium

A HISTORY OF
LONDON COFFEE HOUSES

by
Alex Evans

The history of the humble coffee plant spans well over a thousand years and is as dark and as complex as the brew itself. From its origins in the Horn of Africa to the billion dollar industry it has engendered, coffee has endured a tumultuous and remarkable passage, viewed at various points in its history as both the drink of the masses and as the luxury of Kings; a gift of the Gods and, conversely, a sin by which one could lose one's soul to the Devil. By the time it had arrived on English soil, having travelled from Ethiopia to the Arabian Peninsula via the ancient ports of Mocha and Jidda, before finding its way into Europe and the Mediterranean, coffee had already become an intrinsic part of societal ritual in many parts of the globe, with a legacy of dedicated drinking venues prompted by the first known coffee house, which opened in Constantinople in 1554.

London's premier coffee house began trading on St. Michael's Alley, Cornhill in 1652. Established by Pasqua Rosée, a Greek or Armenian servant to a wealthy English merchant named Daniel Edwards, this seminal London coffee house proved extremely popular, if not for the exotic ritual afforded the drink then for the host of medicinal properties Rosée ascribed it. In a handbill entitled The Vertue of the Coffee Drink, that is displayed in the British Museum, Rosée claimed that coffee could cure gout, scurvy, dropsy, ailments of the lungs and even miscarriages. In line with its perceived medicinal qualities, which were also curiously embellished by some medical professionals, the drink was initially consumed as more of a medicament than a tasty beverage, used to enliven the senses and even provide a safer alternative to opium addiction. Due to poor sanitation and unclean drinking water, a boiled beverage like coffee also became a preferable substitute to wine and ale, whose negative, soporific effects – such as public drunkenness and stomach ailments - were already extremely prevalent in 17th century England.

Accounts of how coffee was prepared and served in these early coffee shops are scarce, though it is reported that coffee was most commonly taken black, without sugar or sweeteners. Coffee roasting would have either taken place in the coffee houses themselves or in premises akin to early coffee roasteries, where beans were roasted over charcoal fires, either in pans or turned on spits using primitive devices such as cylinder roasters, which appeared in London around 1660. Before the advent of coffee mills and grinders, the roasted beans would have then been ground or 'garbled' in a mortar before brewing.

Garraway's Coffee-House.   (From a sketch taken shortly before its demolition)

In December 1660, Samuel Pepys made note of Rosée's coffee house, writing "the first time that ever I was there, and I found much pleasure in it". Indeed, the notoriety that Rosée's venture generated soon became widespread and coffee houses rapidly proliferated.

Borrowing from the traditions of the coffee houses of the Middle East, which had become known as patriarchal social hubs where men met to drink coffee, play chess, make music and to sing, London's first historical coffee houses were abundant with exotic references. Many sold tobacco products, chocolate and tea whilst others provided hookah pipes for customers' use. Signs outside these establishments often depicted middle-eastern imagery and some even had foreign staff or servants to provide a spectacle and authenticity to the surrounds. With names such as the Turk's Head, Jerusalem Coffee House, Morat Ye Great and the Oriental Cigar Divan, these early coffee shops not only satisfied Britain's cultural fascination with the East during the Georgian period, they also fast became as ubiquitous and populated as those in the Muslim world.

London's coffee houses were often large, simply furnished rooms with communal tables that became renowned hotbeds of lively conjecture and debate. The tendency for their patrons' discourse was to provoke the nickname penny universities – so applied because, for the entry fee of a penny, the average layman had access not only to coffee but also to the education afforded by newspapers, pamphlets, discussion and gossip. At a time when the postal service was disorganised, coffee houses also served as stopping points for agents to circulate and impart up-to-the-minute renditions of the city's news. Along with the supporting role coffee houses played in the distribution of London's news and print culture, there were distinct venues for different industries and persuasions. For example, Garraway's on Exchange Alley was rife with merchant trade and the London Stock Exchange began life as a coffee house called Jonathan's, where its owner would put up commodity prices on the wall for his stock-trader clientele. In 1668, Lloyd's Coffee House opened on Tower Street and was to spawn what is today one of the most famous insurance companies in the world. Similarly, Nando's Coffee House, one of the few structural survivors which stands at the Western End of Fleet Street, became the habitué of members of the legal fraternity and so became known colloquially as 'the bar by the bar'.

Neither the Great Fire of 1666, which decimated large portions of London's overcrowded, timber-built habitation, nor the Plague which took the lives of an estimated twenty percent of the city's population the previous year, could halt the spread of coffee houses. Those destroyed were mostly rehoused or rebuilt, funded by their ardent and often wealthy patrons, and those that ceased trading as a consequence did little to prevent altogether new coffee shops from opening. The public's growing appreciation for coffee houses was summed up in 1673, when an anonymous author wrote:

> *"A coffee house is a lay conventicle, good fellowship turned*
> *puritan...whither people come, after toping all day, to purchase at*
> *the expense of their last penny, the repute of sober companions."*

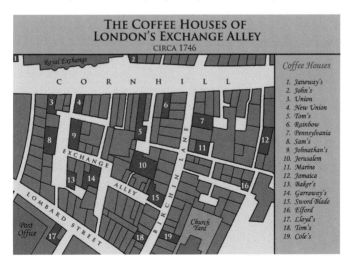

127

However, other sections of the community where less than supportive of London's new-found pastime. In response to the adulation afforded coffee houses and perhaps, in part, their exclusion from them, the Women's Petition Against Coffee was circulated in 1674, which bemoaned their spouse's partaking in 'the excessive use of this drying enfeebling Liquor'. Furthermore, in December 1675, King Charles II responded angrily to the free and potentially treasonous speech that was commonplace within the coffee houses, branding them "seminaries of sedition" and ordering their closure. But the King's proclamation caused uproar within the city, not only from the general public but likewise from royal aides and associates, who advised the King to withdraw his directive. After just eleven days, Charles conceded and lifted the ban, though not before imposing a new taxation of coffee and outlawing the distribution of pamphlets or books within the coffee houses. In retrospect, the King's short-lived prohibition not only increased anti-royalist sentiment but also heightened the popularity of the coffee house; by 1715 they numbered over two thousand in London alone.

The coffee house's propensity for harbouring creativity and radical thinking appears to be a recurring theme throughout history. Certainly, much of the romance and poetical eulogizing they are afforded stems from the literary figures, philosophers and characters who sought refuge within them. Whilst not dissimilar in style to alehouses, coffee houses encouraged sobriety and cogent conversation, and drew personalities whom provided rich material for authors and playwrights short of a character or two. The Sultaness Coffee House, attributed with being the first in London to serve tea, is also notable for being featured in several of Charles Dickens's works, whilst others such as Will's in Covent Garden attracted a crowd of London literati, often referred to as 'The Wits'. Famous authors such as John Dryden, Jonathan Swift and Alexander Pope all frequented West End coffee houses, where satirical verse and heated high-brow hearsay were renowned. By the late 17th century, coffee shops also began to open their doors in other European capital cities such as Paris, Vienna and Hamburg, where they became similarly famous as the offices and hangouts for a host of prominent social figures.

By 1750, coffee was being grown on five continents and its cultivation and export had become a multimillion-pound enterprise. But as coffee and its ritual habitats spread to all four corners of the world, the popularity of coffee houses and coffee drinking in London began to decline. Having been first sold in the coffee houses of London, tea's favour had gradually risen due to influential advertising campaigns by tea's primary importer, the East India Company, and endorsement from the upper classes. This was to prove fortuitous as, following the 1870s epidemic of coffee rust – a lethal fungus that renders the coffee plant unusable – Britain was able to supplant their coffee growing operations in Sri Lanka and India with tea instead. Tea and coffee had also begun being consumed in homes and, unlike coffee, tea required no roasting, grinding and brewing, simply hot water. Exclusive clubs for the social elite had also become popular, starving the coffee shops of their previous custom. All this conspired against coffee's popularity and by the early 19th century, few coffee houses remained in London and many were converted to alehouses or else stopped trading altogether. Whilst coffee continued its tour of the world and was becoming interwoven with the customs of different cities and nations, London's coffee houses had vanished almost as rapidly as they had arisen. It would be several centuries before the fervour surrounding coffee's introduction to London would be rekindled once more.

With the advent of new technologies, the 20th Century marked the birth of a new espresso culture in London when the first Gaggia machine was imported in 1952. By 1956 there were over four hundred cafés inspired by the cosmopolitan coffee culture enjoyed by our Italian counterparts. However, it is only in recent years that cafés in the UK have begun to reflect the speciality coffee movement seen in Australia, New Zealand and some parts of the US. Driven by a new breed of independent, specialty roasters and cafés, London now has one of the greatest coffee scenes in the world with a vitality unparalleled since coffee's arrival in the city some three hundred years ago.

VIVA LA REUSE REVOLUTION

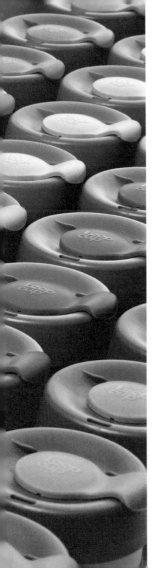

AT KEEPCUP WE ARE ALL ABOUT DOING BETTER

Takeaway coffee that's better for the environment; finding better ways to enjoy the things we love.

Since 2009, KeepCup users have diverted an estimated two billion disposable cups from landfill, saving approximately 750,000 trees from pulp mills. KeepCups are now sold in 26 countries around the world.

KeepCup has been sustainably designed and has won many awards for its innovation and environmental initiative. The KeepCup reuse campaign has been so successful that in our hometown we won the City of Melbourne award for our contribution to sustainability.

KeepCups are available online and at all good cafés.

Stockist enquiries:
+44 207 043 300, info@keepcup.com

Available in:

BETTER & BETTER
KEEPCUP.COM

COFFEE ROASTING

By Lawrence Sinclair
Dark Fluid Coffee

Coffee roasting has two sides, a split personality if you like. There is a romantic side filled with beautiful imagery of 1950s cast iron machinery, pale blue flames, jute sacks and flowing trays of roasted beans. But behind the romance is a world of logistics, record keeping, order and tasting, lots of tasting. For those who care to look, coffee is an enormous and diverse subject, with so many producing countries, types and standards of beans. Coffee roasting holds all the wonder, fascination and challenges of restaurant cooking and the desire to find and roast the best coffee in the world can become an obsession.

Half the challenge of roasting coffee is sourcing the beans. Some, not all, hold the potential for beautiful roasted coffee - all we have to do is find those beans. The better the green coffee, the better the brewed coffee. The way they are produced, graded and processed, along with the altitude at which they are grown, the soil and climate will all affect how the coffee tastes and roasts. However, no combination of these descriptors will actually lead to great coffee. That is to say, high grown coffee is not better than low grown, nor is the Bourbon strain better than the Geisha. They are simply different and for these reasons it's good to remain open minded and choose coffee on taste alone.

Once green beans have been obtained, sample roasting is the way in which we look for a bean's flavor and quality. Small batches are roasted to the same degree - quite light – so not to allow too much influence from the roast level and let the coffee's natural character shine through. The samples are ground and brewed to the same strength and then "cupped" or tasted, often blind. The merits or faults of each coffee are noted and discussed, with sweetness, body, mouth feel and acidity evaluated, amongst other things. Importantly, the roaster can decide from these sample roasts what can be done with a particular coffee if bought in bulk. For example, some are earmarked for espresso blend components and others for light roasted filter coffee.

Essentially, a coffee roaster looks to bring out the best and most unique characteristics in a coffee, as well as achieving a good balance of bitters, acidity and sweetness. If there was a mind-blowing chocolate orange hit noted in the cupping session, the roaster will look to develop a roast profile that maximizes those flavors. A roast profile is a record or plan of how much heat was applied to the beans and for how long. Data logging thermometers are used to read the temperature of both the beans and the drum environment during the roast. If saved and brought to the cupping table they allow us to accurately correlate the taste of the ground, rested beans to the actions we applied in the roasting process. Once a coffee is chosen and a 'best' profile worked out it's time to begin batch roasting.

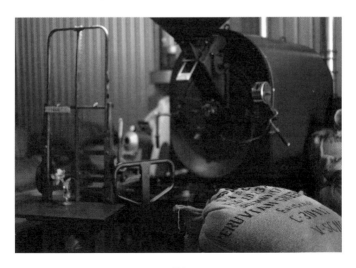

Having organized the green coffee and preheated the roaster, we put the beans in the hopper on top of the roaster and stabilize the heat until it reaches our desired drop temperature. We then pull a tab which drops the beans into a large revolving metal drum with a big gas flame somewhere underneath. The room temperature beans drag the drum temperature down as soon as they enter the drum, and we must turn up the gas to get the heat into the beans quickly.

A few minutes into the roast and the beans have gone a bright yellow and give off a straw like aroma. At this point moisture is being driven off fast and when this drying phase is complete, the beans will start to turn golden brown and the smell of coffee proper will begin to appear. If the early part of the roast is too slow (cool) the beans will become dried and baked as opposed to roasted and the sugars will not caramelize effectively, leading to lackluster brewed coffee. If the heat is applied too aggressively we can get other problems - the beans can scorch leading to that 'chain store' carbon flavour.

After 7 or so minutes the beans are a toasty brown and give off wonderful smells. They hit a point called first crack at about 9 minutes, a violent and noisy expansion of the beans and a rapid discharge of absorbed heat. By this point we will have worked the gas to maintain our desired profile and must continue to adjust the heat and airflow so the coffee develops in the way we intended. A few minutes after the first crack, a second crack takes place. At this point the coffee is quite dark and we may not want to go this far with many coffees, especially those we have acquired because of a particular unique flavour.

As the roast progresses and the beans become darker, the batch, when brewed, will take on the flavors of roasting and the flavours of the individual coffee beans are lost. Towards the end of the roast we monitor the beans' colour, aroma and temperature very closely and small samples are taken from the bean mass to confirm progress. When the roaster judges the batch finished, we pull the door and dump the beans

into a big perforated tray through which cool air passes. A sweeper turns, mixing the beans and speeding up the cooling process. It is important to stop the roasting process quickly to stop the beans from cooking further.

The roasted beans will need a little time to rest, perhaps 4 days to a week for espresso, less for brewed coffee. This allows carbon dioxide, contained within roasted beans, to escape. Espresso brewed too fresh is extremely gassy and hard to pull a nice shot whereas slower brew methods fare better as the gas has had chance to escape. In a month the beans will have become shadows of their fresh roasted glory and so the roaster must get them into the hands and grinders of the brewers and café owners as quickly as possible so they can work their magic.

Coffee roasting is seeing a return to old, before big industry managed to convince the world that vacuum packed coffee could keep for two years and when most towns had a local spinning a Whitmee or an Uno direct flame roaster at a market stall. It is unlikely that the coffee available at this time would pass muster with today's discerning baristas and customers but with traditional methods combining with new innovation and technology it is an exciting time to be coffee roasting. The world has become a small place and the access we have to coffees and the information about them is amazing. The growing interest in fresh roasted, well sourced coffees in the UK means passionate roasters can share their offerings with equally passionate brewers and coffee lovers. Like the cafés listed in this book and their customers.

THE RISE OF
LONDON COFFEE CARTS

by
Derek Lamberton

It is well established that London's flourishing speciality coffee culture has its roots in the pioneering efforts of Monmouth Coffee. Along with an influx of Antipodean aficionados over the past decade, Monmouth has served as a great driving force - inspiring and supporting a generation of baristas, roasters and coffee drinkers across London. But perhaps more influential, and certainly less acknowledged, has been a cast of characters willing to expose themselves to some of London's least desirable elements in the name of speciality coffee. This group includes many of London's most vocal, intelligent and entertaining proponents of food artisanship. They are, of course, the coffee cart baristas.

'It all began with a builder's trolley', says Gwilym Davies with a laugh. In 1999, when Borough Market reopened for trading, Monmouth rolled out what might be considered a coffee cart, consisting of little more than a crate secured to the top of a trolley. Above the crate was Monmouth's original La Marzocco Linea and a filter rack. Behind the cart were Davies, now co-owner of Prufrock and the 2009 World Barista Champion, and Jorge Fernandez, co-owner of Fernandez & Wells, who until then had worked together at a coffee cart named Cuppuccino serving Monmouth in Clapham Junction. Monmouth Coffee would eventually move their business indoors, but Davies would move on to Columbia Road where he permanently changed the landscape of coffee in London.

Columbia Road Flower Market is where many Londoners first discovered speciality coffee. Davies originally set up in the courtyard off Ezra Street in 2003 using the same espresso machine from Borough Market on top of a replica cart. Wedged in next to a popular bacon sandwich stall, Davies's cart built up a loyal following with queues running half an hour deep. In 2008, this Sunday cart became the first wholesale customer for an up-and-coming local roastery named Square Mile. Caught off guard by the change, many customers voiced a sense of betrayal at Davies, not realising that one of Square Mile's founders - James Hoffmann - was often there alongside Davies making their coffee. But Davies, knowing that a cart was the perfect setting to make such a change, maintained his confidence and explained his reasoning.

'It's all about transparency', says Davies, describing work behind a coffee cart. 'There are no barriers, meaning you are completely exposed.' The intimacy of a cart allows for casual interaction between a barista and customer. Every step of making a coffee is on display with customers watching from all angles. The benefits to this setting are mutual: the customer witnesses the process and is more likely to ask questions and provide feedback; and the barista is able to gauge the customer's reaction, answer questions and provide details about the coffee. The impact of the cart on the growth of speciality coffee in London cannot therefore be underestimated. More than perhaps any other influence, the cart has educated casual coffee drinkers and shifted palates towards lighter roasts and speciality grade beans.

Regular customers of Davies's Columbia Road cart would have been served by an unprecedented level of talent. Future World Barista Champions - including Davies, Hoffmann and Stephen Morrissey - were all regulars behind the cart. With them were baristas like Tim Williams, now director of operations at Workshop Coffee Co., Jeremy Challender, co-owner of Prufrock and other leading baristas from across London and around the world, many of whom would hop out of the queue to pull shots and texture milk whilst others grabbed a bacon sandwich. Stories of barista throwdowns and impromptu competitions abound. Needless to say, the loyal customers eventually accepted Square Mile's roasts and London began its ascent onto the world coffee stage.

Other early carts - notably Whitecross Street and Strutton Ground - have also served as starting points for some of London's most influential baristas, roasters and entrepreneurs. Davies and Challender moved to Whitecross Street in 2007, which they ran until they set up a machine in Present under their Prufrock banner in 2009. The successful partnership of Fabio Ferreira and Robert Robinson, co-owners of Notes, began on Strutton Ground in 2008 at a cart that became Flat Cap. They now trade at numerous locations - both carts and cafés - across London and attract some of the best baristas in Europe.

Lee Harte spent time working on both Whitecross Street and Strutton Ground learning from the best, before setting up his own cart in Fortune Park called Giddy Up. He now runs a popular spread of carts in Angel, Guildhall and Shoreditch, alongside Fortune Park. With years of experience producing coffee outdoors, Harte knows the trade as well as anyone. Half jokingly he describes the cart barista as a 'special beast' who is unlike the café barista, who 'has soft hands and enjoys warm breakfasts'. Harte also speaks of the critical role cart baristas have played in the growth of quality coffee in London with their easy-to-approach manner. 'I love the way people can just wander over without the big moment of entering a café for the first time,' Harte says.

Rob Lockyear, now managing sales at Allpress Espresso, manned a cart called Brewed Boy on Rupert Street in Soho from 2010 to 2011. Like Harte he also points to the hard-nosed characteristics needed to serve a killer coffee with a smile, despite chapped hands, the rain, the snow, and an unbelievable array of hardships from 'being robbed and punched to figuring out where to source electricity and what to do with stolen property suddenly stashed in your cart by professional shoplifters'. Lockyear describes his experience working behind a cart as 'the best and worst thing I have ever done'. But despite the daily drama often involved, people like Lockyear and Harte are able to reach a customer that would not necessarily walk into a speciality coffee shop without first tasting speciality coffee.

London's coffee carts have spawned world barista champions, leading speciality roasters, café owners and, of course, more carts. Today, quality coffee carts can be found in every corner of the capital. Lawrence Sinclair, a cart veteran, runs the incredibly popular Dark Fluid cart every Saturday in Brockley Market. Merito sets up in Swiss Cottage during the week and Broadway Market on Saturdays. Flat Cap, Giddy Up and Bean About Town carts are numerous, while newcomers like Craft Coffee, Terrone and Black & White Coffee Co. attract loyal followings with their quality approach.

Although carts serving coffee have undoubtedly wheeled across London streets for years, in many respects it was Monmouth's Borough Market trolley that marked the beginning of London's current coffee obsession. The level of talent that has been involved in the growth of the carts spawned by this makeshift trolley is remarkable. Today, coffee cart baristas continue to work in a transparent manner that attracts both new customers and aficionados. In this unique position on the front line, they continue to wield an unrivalled influence on the growth of speciality coffee customers. Or, as Giddy Up's Harte describes it, they continue 'tearing down walls'.

HARIO | JAPANESE COFFEE EQUIPMENT
YOUR DELICIOUS COFFEE
BREWED TO ORDER

WWW.HARIOGLASS.COM   SALES@BREWEDBYHAND.CO.UK

BREWING
WHAT YOU NEED

1 A set of digital scales for weighing out your coffee and water. We recommend a versatile scale like the one pictured, as this allows you to time and weigh simultaneously.

2 A kettle for boiling or heating your water to the correct temperature. This particular model has a gooseneck spout for easier pouring, a definite advantage when using the V60 pour over brew method.

3 A grinder. Whether using a hand grinder – like the one pictured – or an electric one, be sure it has burrs as opposed to blades, which will grind rather slice your coffee beans.

4 Some good coffee. This should be bought with your own taste in mind but we advise buying coffee with a roast date and information on the bag about the region, farm and producer of that particular coffee. Provenance usually ensures a higher grade of coffee in the bag.

AEROPRESS

Devised in 2005 by Alan Adler, the Aeropress is a simple and versatile way for brewing at home and can be used in a variety of different ways. When used correctly, the Aeropress is ideal for single cup brewing, either at home or in a café. Below are our guidelines for brewing with the Aeropress but remember to experiment with your own times and brew ratios to suit your tastes.

1. Start by placing your filter paper into the Aeropress cap and rinsing with plenty of hot water – this will help to eliminate any of the residual paper flavor. Also preheat the Aeropress at this point if so desired.

2. Grind 18 grams of coffee to the texture of course sand. This grind setting may also be referred to as a drip filter setting, or roughly half way between espresso and French press.

3. Place the Aeropress upside down on the scale, add your ground coffee and tare.

4. Add 200-230 grams of 85-90 degree filtered water, starting your timer as soon as the water comes into contact with the ground coffee. Make sure that all the coffee grounds are wetted.

5. After 1 minute of pre-infusion time with the cap off, use a stirrer to agitate the grounds. The more you stir, the stronger the coffee will end up, so be careful not to over-do it.

6. Let it steep for another minute.

7. Add the cap to the Aeropress and flip it onto your cup or jug. Begin to plunge slowly, without excessive force. If you find the Aeropress hard to push down, grind the coffee more coarsely next time. This should take no more than 30 seconds.

8. Serve and enjoy. Remember to let the coffee cool before drinking so as to let those flavours shine through.

CAFETIERE

Also known as the French Press, plunger or coffee press, the cafetiere was patented by Milanese designer Attilio Calimani in 1929 and is perhaps the easiest and cheapest way of brewing coffee at home.

1. Preheat your cafetiere with hot water. Remember to use filtered or bottled water to ensure the best results when brewing coffee.

2. Grind your coffee to a coarse, even grind, the same texture as that pictured. Depending on the size of your cafetiere and the amount of brewed coffee you want, you'll need a varying amount of ground coffee but we suggest using a ratio of 75 grams of coffee per litre of water.

3. Empty the water from your preheated cafetierre and add your ground coffee.

4. Add your hot water – preferably around 30 seconds off the boil – and begin your timer.

5. Let it brew for 3 minutes with the plunger lid off. Stir vigorously and let stand for a further minute.

6. At 4 minutes, remove the crust of ground coffee on top with a spoon - this lessens the amount of grinds that will end up in your coffee and produces a cleaner taste.

7. Add the lid and begin to plunge slowly. If you find it hard to push down, you've probably ground your coffee too finely.

8. Once you have plunged all the way down, decant or pour out your coffee straight away - if left in the cafetiere it will continue to brew, resulting in bitter, over-extracted coffee.

DRIP FILTER

Drip filters, filter cones or pour overs are one of the most common ways to brew coffee at home and are also used extensively in cafés throughout London. Being one of the gentlest brewing methods, drip filters produce well-rounded cups of coffee with great clarity of flavour. Some drip filters, such as the V60 (pictured) or the Chemex, employ filter papers whereas others use gauze or cloth filters, which allow varying amounts of fines and coffee oils through.

1. For a one cup V60 filter weigh out 15 grams of coffee and set to a medium grind like that in the picture. For larger amounts we recommend using a generic ratio of 60-70 grams of coffee per litre.

2. Fold the filter paper along the edge and place into the V60.

3. Rinse the filter paper thoroughly with hot water to eliminate residual paper flavours. Doing this warms both your brewer and your cup or carafe.

4. Add your ground coffee. You may want to make a small indentation at the centre of the coffee with your finger, to prevent the dripper from clogging.

5. Cover the coffee with your hot water – around 30 seconds off the boil - and let bloom for 45 seconds.

6. Pour over the rest of your water, making small outward circles from the centre and ensuring that all of the ground coffee is being wetted. Keep the coffee bed low in the cone, adding the water slowly and in small increments.

7. Water should disappear across the whole bed simultaneously for an even extraction, which should last approximately 2 minutes 30 seconds.

8. Once all the coffee has dripped through let the coffee cool in the cup or carafe slightly before serving.

LONDON'S BEST

· ·

COFFEE

COFFEE GLOSSARY

ACIDITY

One of the three principal tastes employed by professional coffee tasters in detailing a particular coffee or blend. When used in coffee terms acidity is a desirable characteristic, providing a bright, vibrant quality.

AMERICANO *(Caffè Americano)*

A term coined during World War II when American GIs stationed in Europe would add hot water to their espresso to replicate the coffee they were accustomed to drinking in the United States. Essentially the term still means an espresso with added hot water.

ARABICA *(Coffea Arabica)*

The most widely grown species of coffee tree, Arabica accounts for approximately 70% of the world's coffee and thrives when grown at high elevation in cooler and drier climates. It is generally seen as superior in terms of taste and quality to other coffee species. The plant was originally indigenous to Ethiopia but the name Arabica is derived from the Arabian Peninsula, having been exported there in large quantities. It is believed to be the first coffee species to be cultivated, with evidence of its growth dating back well over 1000 years.

BARISTA

The Italian term for bar person which now connotes a professional coffee maker or expert.

BLEND

A combination of two or more coffee subspecies (such as Bourbon or Typica) that are blended together. It can lead to a more balanced coffee flavour or flavours that are greater than the sum total of its parts.

BREW TIME

Contact time between water and coffee. The guideline for a correctly brewed espresso is between 20 and 30 seconds, though the exact times are dictated by roasting dates, blend components and many other variables.

CORTADO

A traditional Spanish coffee made up of an espresso shot cut with a small amount of steamed milk without much foam. A Spanish piccolo.

CREMA

The golden foam that covers the surface of an espresso shot. Crema is made by the pressurised brew water forcing its way through the coffee bed.

CUPPING

The procedure employed by coffee tasters in order to evaluate samples of coffee beans, the key evaluation characteristics being aroma, acidity, body and flavour.

DOSAGE

The amount of ground coffee used to produce an espresso shot. Typically around 7-11 grams of coffee is used for a single espresso shot and 16-25 grams for a double.

ESPRESSO

The basis of most coffee beverages served in cafés, an espresso shot is produced when hot water is forced at high pressure through a compressed bed of finely ground coffee in an espresso machine. This generally takes between 20 and 30 seconds and yields 20-30 mls of liquid. Much like the English word 'express', the term refers to the speed of its preparation, when compared to other coffee brewing methods.

FLAT WHITE

An espresso based beverage invented in Australia or New Zealand prepared by pouring steamed milk with a thin layer of microfoam over a single or double shot of espresso.

GRIND

Whole coffee beans are ground to different sizes depending on the brew method. As a rule, the larger or courser the grind, the longer the brew time. The espresso grind is small or fine and takes up to approximately 30 seconds, whereas the cafetiere grind is coarser and is brewed for approximately 4 minutes.

LATTE *(Caffè Latte)*

Literally translated from the Italian for 'coffee and milk', a latte is a single espresso shot combined with foamed milk and is usually served in a glass.

LATTE ART

The creation of a pattern or design on the surface of a coffee beverage by either free pouring steamed milk over an espresso shot or etching designs onto the finished coffee using a coffee stirrer. Common types of latte art are the Rosetta or the heart shape.

MICRO-LOT COFFEES

A small lot of coffee that has benefited from conditions, such as soil, shade or selective picking, that has been isolated in one particular area of a farm. These conditions can create a unique character to the coffee which sets it apart from the rest of the crop in terms of quality. Due to the extra preparation required, their resulting quality and the small scale of their production, micro-lot coffees also fetch higher prices.

OVER EXTRACTED

Bitter, harsh and unpleasant flavours that are the result of the contact time between water and coffee grounds being too long or brew water that is too hot.

PICCOLO

Literally meaning 'small' in Italian, a Piccolo is a smaller variant of the latte. Consists of an espresso or ristretto shot, topped with steamed milk and is usually served in a small glass at a 1:1 ratio of espresso to milk.

RISTRETTO

A "restricted" espresso. A ristretto is richer and more intense than a traditional espresso shot due to the smaller volume of brew water in comparison to coffee.

ROBUSTA *(Coffea Canephora)*

Behind Arabica, Robusta is the other primary coffee species to be used commercially. Unlike Arabica, Robusta has a shallow root system and grows a robust tree or shrub that is less susceptible to pests and disease, requires less care in growing and can flourish at low altitudes. The typical yield of Robusta is twice that of Arabica and the resulting coffee contains twice as much caffeine, though less complex flavours. Robusta is often used as a filler in lower-quality filter blends and instant coffees.

SINGLE ORIGIN COFFEE

Coffee from one country. Single origin coffees can capture the essence of a particular country due to variants such as soil, altitude and climate specific to that growing area. Within single origin definitions there are also single estate coffees, which refers to an area or estate within that country of origin, akin to wine regions.

SPECIALTY COFFEE

A term used to denote a gourmet or premium coffee that has achieved a 'specialty' classification having scored 80 points or above on the one hundred point grading scale employed by traders and coffee associations. Specialty coffee has also come to represent a wider range of meaning, encompassing methods of coffee preparation, industry practice and café culture.

TAMP/TAMPING

The method by which loose coffee grounds are compressed and compacted into a portafilter basket in preparation for brewing espresso.

UNDER EXTRACTED

When contact time, temperature or turbulence is insufficient to fully extract desirable flavours from coffee.

THANKS

Ben Townsend, Andrew Tolley, James Lambie, Bahar Tafti, Paul Radin, Nick Coates, A.J. Kinnell, James Phillips, Tim Williams, Robert Robinson, Peter Dore-Smith, Jeremy Torz, Steven Macatonia, Gavin Fernback and to all the café owners, coffee roasters and baristas who have made this book possible.

Derek Lamberton would personally like to thank Laura, DunneFrankowski and the teams at Browns of Brockley and Prufrock.

Vespertine Press would also like to acknowledge the help and guidance of Four Corners Print, Lloyd Price, B.P. Evans, Susan and Robin Sykes, Karen Bouchard, Meg, Holly, Cal McLeod, Wes Goatley, Richard Grills, all Brighton coffee folk and everyone at the mews.

This book is dedicated to Monty

STAY IN TOUCH

 @cafeguides

 @vespertinepress

 facebook.com/vespertinepress

www.vespertinepress.co.uk

SPECIALIST CITY GUIDES

Vespertine PRESS

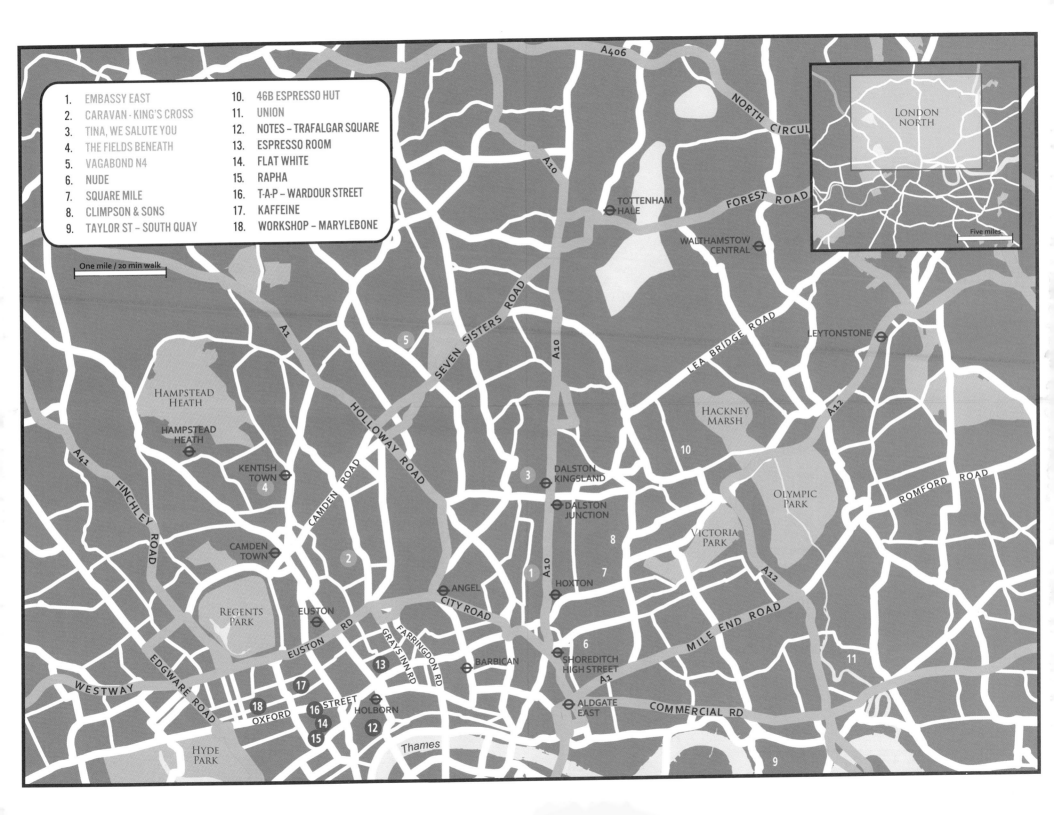

1. EMBASSY EAST
2. CARAVAN - KING'S CROSS
3. TINA, WE SALUTE YOU
4. THE FIELDS BENEATH
5. VAGABOND N4
6. NUDE
7. SQUARE MILE
8. CLIMPSON & SONS
9. TAYLOR ST – SOUTH QUAY
10. 46B ESPRESSO HUT
11. UNION
12. NOTES – TRAFALGAR SQUARE
13. ESPRESSO ROOM
14. FLAT WHITE
15. RAPHA
16. T-A-P – WARDOUR STREET
17. KAFFEINE
18. WORKSHOP – MARYLEBONE

One mile / 20 min walk

LONDON
NORTH

Five miles

LONDON SOUTH

Five miles

One mile / 20 min walk

1. TAYLOR ST – MONUMENT
2. CURATORS
3. ASSOCIATION
4. DOSE ESPRESSO
5. NOTES COFFEE BARROW
6. WORKSHOP – CLERKENWELL
7. PRUFROCK
8. LOOK MUM, NO HANDS
9. PROTEIN BY DUNNEFRANKOWSKI
10. SALVATION JANE
11. OZONE COFFEE
12. GIDDY UP FLORIPA
13. CRAFT COFFEE
14. MONMOUTH – DOCKLEY ROAD
15. FEDERATION
16. BROWNS OF BROCKLEY
17. DARK FLUID
18. BIRDHOUSE